Through raw vulnerability
is refreshing and real. Kay
that no matter what our pa
a life of adventure and amazement--when we give
God our one and only life.

Eileen Wilder
Bestselling Author, The Brave Body Method

I confess: I love stories. Stories reveal reality. They offer
perspectives we often fail to grasp in our hi-tech, multi-task,
all-about-ourselves world. Stories open windows for us to see
from a fresh view. Stories can also kick open the doors and
lure us toward a new vision, a new world, a new future.

Kayla Buckner's book, Rescued Royal, does that. Her
authenticity merges with her compassion as she presents the
stories from her heart.

The subtitle gives us a glimpse of where Kayla's story takes
us: Sex, Drugs, & Jesus - Walking Through Hell & Colliding
with Love. Does that get your attention? Her story invites you
to learn about her, but also to collide with love in the middle
of your own painful story.

Read her story. Feel her grief, denial, decisions, counseling,
and healing by Papa God. And realize that Papa God is here for
you. Welcome Him into your story. Like Kayla's story, yours
will never be the same.

You'll love her story. And I hope you'll welcome Papa God's
love into your story.

Chris Maxwell,
Author, Speaker, Pastor

{A True Story}

Rescued Royal: Sex, Drugs, & Jesus

Walking Through Hell & Colliding with Love

Kayla Buckner

Cover design: Bailey Rushlow – Nashville, TN
Author Photo ALB Photography Designs, Gainesville GA

Now Available for Amazon Kindle
Rescued Royal: Sex, Drugs, & Jesus – Walking Through Hell & Colliding with Love is available for download on your tablet, smart phone or other mobile device, to carry wherever you go.
You can also use it as a reference on your desktop or laptop computer with the free Kindle App.
Search the Amazon Kindle Store for *Rescued Royal: Sex, Drugs, & Jesus – Walking Through Hell & Colliding with Love* or go directly to http://amazon.com/rescuedroyal

Rescued Royal: Sex, Drugs, & Jesus – Walking Through Hell & Colliding with Love available at Amazon.com
after January 29, 2017.

Email: rescuedroyal@gmail.com

www.rescuedroyal.com

Contents

To my beautiful friend, Bailey Rushlow.

I cannot think of a more true and beautiful
representation of authenticity than a girl
that refuses to be anyone but who
she was created to be!

You inspire me to dive deeper, pursue Jesus
relentlessly, and challenge me to be only
who I was created to be, myself.

I am so grateful that our worlds collided and I
am beyond honored to call you friend!
You make the world a better place.
You are changing history!

I love you big, Bails!

Chapter One

Beautifully Broken

I was so scared.
White walls surrounded me when I walked through the doorframe towards him.

All I wanted to do was curl up into a ball, close my eyes, and pretend that it was all a dream. I felt so small and none of this made sense. My mind was struggling to connect with the reality of my past.

Was it 1989 or 1988? I can't remember! There are so many memories attached to those years, memories that stirred up dark feelings of shame, hate, anger, bitterness, confusion, and fear. The enemy did his best to ruin me, taint my heart, and shut me down. I can admit that he did a really good job at it for a while - rendering me a person that hell didn't have to worry about for quite some time.

1

There is very little that I remember about my life before the age of 7 or 8, or at least until February 18th, 2015. For most of my life I wondered why I could not remember those years. I fought several times to stir up the memories but failed every time. I could not decide if it was fear that was keeping me from remembering - fear of what I might discover - or if it was because something so traumatic had happened to me that my brain literally slammed the door closed on all that had occurred and buried the key with it.

One of the earliest memories I have is of August 9th, 1992 when I received the news that my baby sister had arrived. My mom had given birth to a beautiful, energetic little girl who would become my world... but I was so mad. My frail little heart was hurt because I wasn't there when she was born.

My 7-year-old mind could not figure out why Mom did not wait for me to get back home for the birth. I had been sent off with a group from church to Myrtle Beach the week before. I was excited about getting to go on one of my first trips without the rest of my family, but I was "supposed" to be in the hospital room while Abby was gracing the world with her beautiful presence. That is what the plan had been. At the time, I didn't understand the biological process that came with giving birth. I just wanted to be there when she came and I was convinced that there was a hidden reason I had missed the big moment.

Even though missing the birth was unavoidable, I still believed that it was my fault for not being there. I would run it over and over in my head saying, "I should have been there!" I felt that it was my fault I had not been at the hospital that day.

The enemy crept in during the early years of my life and planted destructive lies that I would hold onto for years and years to come. Blaming myself for not being good enough or important enough became a daily theme in my life. It all began around the age of 4 or 5, but I couldn't pinpoint why until quite a few years later. What would soon be uncovered changed my life in an unexpected and radical way.

Shame & Blame

Shame and blame was the game that I was entangled in and I didn't even know it. It was exhausting and far from fun but it was my normal. I stepped into a victim mentality not understanding the destructive implications this would have later on in my life. I truly believed I was a failure. From a very young age the enemy had been throwing rocks at my life - rocks that had continued to get bigger and heavier as time went on.

Re-living old memories can be fun and exhilarating, bringing tears of joy and happiness, laughter, and even inspiring the pursuit of new memory-creating moments.

Other memories bring up pain, anger, and fear, sometimes to such a pain-filled degree that we are incapable of remembering until they are specifically triggered. They get shut out, blocked off and buried; the keys are thrown away in hopes we'll never visit that "graveside" ever again.

Those types of memories hide behind a thick black curtain and haunt our mind, leaving us with a "sense" that something is there... like a nagging, wordless question. It may simply be from fear of what we may come face to face with that our mind forgets in order to cope.

February 18th 2015, I remember that day like it was yesterday. This date will forever be with me because it revealed a big ugly mark in my history. I could see him standing in front of me. I was toe to toe with him. My forehead at his waist, the bottom of his square silver belt buckle reflecting back at me, the little girl that stood in front of him.

I didn't know who he was. My mind raced within the memory, desperate to understand what was happening, desperate to know who this man was standing before me. The thoughts that sprinted through that little girl's mind - through MY mind - were horrible and disturbing.

"Please don't! Please don't unzip them!"

The building black cloud of fear for what was coming next attacked my thoughts. I could see his right hand reach over to the zipper on his dark blue denim pants. His hands were much older than mine. They could have been a father's hands.   His zipper glides all the way down.

Nothing.
Silence.
Frozen.
Numb.
Scared.

The deafening silence that rang in my ears jolted through my body like electricity. It was as if someone had taken a black sheet and suddenly draped it between the memory and I.

EMDR was over.

EMDR is Eye Movement Desensitization and Reprocessing therapy that helps to process memory in trauma patients or someone with PTSD. EMDR is similar to what happens during dreaming, or the REM (rapid eye movement) cycle in sleep. Because I could not recall most of my memory before the age of 7, my counselor, Alissa, used EMDR to help me recall the memories and process them in a healthy way to help me heal.

When we began, I was completely unaware of what may emerge. The memories did not all come immediately or all together. And to be honest, I was skeptical at what was surfacing in my mind. I was not sure that EMDR would help or even work. However, Papa God nudged me to dive in with all that I had. I wanted to face the things that had held me back, let Him strip me down to nothing, and rebuild my history. I was desperate. He used EMDR to expose the root of so many things that I had buried deep, beginning to rebuild the ruins within me.

> *The Spirit of the Lord God is upon me, because the Lord has anointed me to bring good news to the afflicted; He has sent me to bind up the brokenhearted, to proclaim liberty to captives and freedom to prisoners; to proclaim the favorable year of the Lord and the day of vengeance of our God; to comfort all who mourn, to grant those who mourn in Zion, giving them a garland instead of ashes, the oil of gladness instead of mourning, the mantle of praise instead of a spirit of fainting. So they will be called oaks of righteousness, the planting of the Lord, that He may be glorified. Then they will rebuild the ancient ruins, they will raise up the former devastations; and they will repair the ruined cities, the desolations of many generations.*
>
> Isaiah 61:1-4

Isaiah 61 is a chapter in the Word that I have always loved. At that time, it was also the very essence of what was happening in my life going through EMDR. The ruins of my life, my heart, were being rebuilt in my soul and my spirit.

My counselor, Alissa, embodied the hope of Isaiah 61 well, and I prayed that one day I would be able to speak this and believe it about myself too; I prayed that I would be able to walk fully in who I was created to be, and truly believe that I was created for greatness beyond myself.

After this particular EMDR session that took place February 18th, I looked up at Alissa with what I am sure was a terrified and very confused look on my face. I shook and trembled inside while asking myself the question, "Where did he go?" I did not recognize who that belt belonged to...but those hands. I had knots in the pit of my stomach that told me I probably knew who this man was. The thought ran through my head, "Surely it is not who I think it is." Although, it would be no surprise considering this man's radiant past of "mishaps" and "mistakes."

I could feel the terror buzzing through my body, but I could not wrap my brain around what I had just re-lived. I questioned if what I was remembering was reality or if it was something that I made up in my mind, but my physical reaction proved otherwise. It was like my body remembered more than my head did. An influx of emotion hit me like a river bursting through a floodgate. Anger, hurt, pain, confusion, and fear tore through me and I felt as though I was drowning.

According to psychological study, the human body can feel and react to trauma and forgotten memory before the brain can actually catch up and reveal the truth of that trauma. It is called PTSD. I had been studying psychology in school and learning about this type of trauma at the time, but I still swirled in confusion. Was this really happening to me? How could I have PTSD? How could I be THAT person?!

Admitting that such a horrible thing had happened to me was not something I was prepared for. I had heard of things like this happening to others. I had even empathized and sympathized with strangers and friends when hearing about the unimaginable horrors that had happened to them. But now I was sitting in that seat, no longer only an observer, and it hurt. It was scary as hell. I did not want to be a statistic. But as much as I hated it, as much as I wanted to believe otherwise - this was now my reality.

I sat in Alissa's office day after day fighting both to remember and to heal from something I had very little understanding of and absolutely no control over. I wanted to cry, run, scream, and hide...but with every bit of who I was, I wanted to settle my past even more. In order to move forward with my life, I had to face these things head on.

During this time, one of the biggest lessons I learned was that I could not have done it without Papa God! It was not easy. In fact, it was one of the most challenging things I have ever come to face. Memories began to unlock and emerge from the closets I had barricaded in the back of my mind. Every time I went to see Alissa I would take one more step in pushing my way through the halls of my memories, and I would remember a little more. Emotions emerged that I had fought so hard to keep on lockdown.

I prayed. I prayed so hard.

The memories that began to flow through my mind wrenched my heart with each passing image and thought. The images of this man on top of me, of being pulled closer to him, of him telling me it was okay because he loved me, caused my stomach to turn in ways I was unaware it could do so. Feelings of fear and confusion took over. Being summoned to come closer while being asked if I loved him back rang in my ears and I wanted it quiet. I was 29 years old taking up residence in a 4-year-old little girl's vision, thoughts, feelings, and trembling and I wanted out.

My heart broke for that little girl who had no control over what was happening. I couldn't save her. I couldn't protect her. But I could feel her heart, hear her thoughts, and feel her trembling, but I could do nothing for her. That little girl was me and that pissed me off!

Why couldn't I have "happy" memories like everyone else!?! What had I done to deserve such brutal abuse? This was not love!! How could it be!?! Why was it allowed to happen to me? I did not understand why. If God was such a good Father, why did I have to go through something so horrific - especially as an innocent and helpless child?

I cried. I shook. I hid. I dissociated. I screamed at times. There were even times I prayed for it to all end. I didn't want to remember anymore. It hurt too much.

I was remembering his face, his touch, his hands, his breath. I was remembering how much I loved him as a child but then my 29 year old self began to recognize just how abnormal our relationship was when I was too little to understand the perversion that took place in it.

This man was one of my favorite people but he turned out to be one of the most dangerous in my life. He blended quite well, I must say. He was a leader, a man that others looked up to, and a worship pastor. This man led worship at the church I grew up in, the church my whole family attended, and the church that my Pawpaw pastored. This man, the man that I once looked up to, adored, and would do anything for as a child, turned out to be the main event of my biggest nightmare.

In the process of remembering what happened to that little girl's innocence, I also began to notice the cruel ways those unknown memories had woven themselves into my current existence, as if designed to steal my future.

But why? Why do things happen the way they do? Everything happens for a reason, right? At least that is what I have been told my whole life. Is that saying even true? Then why do horrible things have to happen?

As I sat in my bedroom one night about a year ago, my heart began to burn. To be honest, I did not understand completely what was happening but I knew that it was not the enemy. As I sat in the floor in tears on the phone with a friend, she began praying over me and then explained what she was seeing - Papa God in the room with me on several occasions as a little girl. The times I was being abused sexually, the times I was being abused mentally, emotionally, and spiritually. She saw Him screaming at the people that were hurting me. He was screaming at them, pleading with them, wanting so badly to make it stop, but because we are each given free will, there are certain boundaries He has set up for Himself and He could not cross those boundaries. Even though that sounds like He couldn't protect me, nothing could be farther from the truth! He did protect me. He kept me. He held me when I was at my weakest. He pursued me so fiercely that even though I went years through what seemed like hell, I could not help but surrender myself to Him! He made me believe He actually loves me! And He loves you, too!

As she explained what she was seeing, she also explained how He was mending my heart. He was holding my heart and kissing it whole. The scars from the wounds to my heart were healing.

I fully believe that if my history had been different I wouldn't be the person that I am today. I understand that God never intended for those terrible things to invade my life, but that He is now redeeming all that has been stolen, and that He has and will use my history to be part of the change in other people's lives.

He can and will do the same for you if you will allow Him

To those that are reading this right now that have experienced deep pain and wounding, know that when you were going through those things, or if you happen to be right in the middle of that situation now, regardless of what "that" situation is, Papa God wants nothing more than to sweep you up and protect you! Our idea of protection and His idea of protection may differ, but it in no way means that His protection is not over your life! He wants nothing more than to protect your heart! And even when it doesn't seem like that is what is happening, you were kept and you *are* kept. You are pursued, you are wanted, you are desired in the purest of ways, and you are loved beyond your understanding!

Discretion will guard you, understanding will watch over you.

PROVERBS 2:11

A beautiful friend reminded me of this verse a while back; she reminded me that even through this recount of the things that I have walked through in my short 31 years of life, discretion will guard me and understanding will watch over me. It is so easy to get wrapped up in our past, to let the things that happened to us form our identity, to run from sharing, or to cave under the heaviness that the enemy will try to lay on you. However, Papa God has set in place a way to pursue wisdom in a way that will not only teach us how to guard ourselves against the enemy but to understand how to stand and fight with the heart of a soldier!

No Such Thing As Coincidence!

I do not believe in coincidence, luck, or chance. I believe in destiny and purpose.

So then, what is the purpose for everything that happens in our lives? Sometimes there is no "right" answer for what happens to us. However, I have found that there is an answer to one thing, and that is how will you let the things that happened to you cause change in the world rather than ruin the precious life you were given?

My answer is not easy for everyone to grasp, and some may not agree, but this is where Papa God has brought me. I refuse to let my past define me. I refuse to let those that hurt me have control over my heart any longer. I refuse to let what has happened control me. I refuse to let hell keep me from walking into my destiny!

I choose to pursue a life of real and raw vulnerability. My goals are to make a difference, to see lives changed, to shift atmospheres with the presence of Holy Spirit, and to change the world by showing others that they are not alone; to show they were created for greatness beyond themselves. My biggest goal, however, is to share Jesus in everything that I do!

Life is about loving with the heart of God and allowing Him to impact a world of hurting people through us. It is about surrender and letting Him use your past to change the world. Let me be clear, you don't have to have a horrible past in order to make an impact, meet people where they are, or change the world!

******

Everyone has a story.
A unique story designed and fashioned to them.
No one's story is the same but the beauty that can be found through the trial and testing is immeasurable.

******

Genesis 50:20 says, *"As for you, you meant evil against me, but God meant it for good in order to bring about his present result, to preserve many people alive."*

The truth is that Satan wants nothing more than to destroy you and there is nothing that he will not try in order to take you out. But God created you to ruin hell, not to be ruined by hell. The enemy will fight dirty, and will try to use your past against you. He will try dumping shame on you, but that is not something you were created to carry.

So many of us have been through what others cannot imagine, but we are not alone and our story does not end with our past. Your past is simply that: your past. Papa God can use it to shift atmospheres, bring healing, and change the world if you will let Him.

You are NOT damaged goods.
You are NOT worthless.
You are NOT forgotten.
And your past does NOT determine your destiny!
ONLY Papa God does!

Destiny demands surrender.
What are you willing to surrender?

Chapter Two

Formed and Fashioned

She scooped me up and sat me on the back of the pew, asking "Do you want to know Jesus? REALLY know Him, for yourself?"

"He loves you so much, with everything that He has, and He wants you, Kayla. Do you want to be His?" she asked. I was only about 7 years old but I understood this question more than I could express, and it resonated deep inside me.

With tears streaming down my cheek I looked at her shaking my head as the small but powerful word escaped my mouth: "Yes!" I declared.

That's all I had ever wanted but I was afraid to tell anyone because I did not feel like I was allowed to make any decisions on my own. I walked up to the front of the church with my head down and prayed my prayer. I did not know how people would react but something in me

17

did not care in that moment. I knew things would be different, even at that young age.

Growing up in church as a pastor's granddaughter presented several challenges... My dad's father, Pawpaw, was the pastor of a Pentecostal holiness/non-denomination church in Georgia where I was born and raised for a good portion of my childhood.

In the beginning of his ministry, he was incredibly connected with Holy Spirit. He walked in an anointing that could only be given by Father God. He walked in and demonstrated power that caused demons to shutter and the dead to awaken. But the church became incredibly legalistic in many ways over time, and Pawpaw allowed pride to creep in and take control. Religion drowned out relationship and distraction made it impossible to realize what was happening in plain sight.

My entire family attended because it was simply expected, a kind of family law. My grandfather had a way about him; he was a controlling man and no one ever seemed to be able to tell him no.

So many things went on in the four walls of that church. I spent more time at the church and my grandparent's house (all located on the same piece of property) than I spent anywhere else. I was involved in every aspect of the church that I could be at such a young age. It was all that I knew.

I did not feel, however, that I was allowed to speak unless spoken to, and I felt that I had to be perfect in every way. I did not know how to be my own person. I did not know that was allowed or even possible.

I dreamed of being heard, but rarely felt that I was. I believed that regardless of how I felt, it didn't matter. I was to put on a happy little smile for everyone. We had to be (or at least look like) the perfect family. If I disappointed them I got in trouble, at least this is how I felt. That is how I saw the world– as if I had a reputation to protect.

Striving for Perfection

I think too often we feel the need to be perfect. We chase after this idea of what or who we think we should be rather than who we actually are, who we were created to be. Striving for perfection, by the world's definition, creates a false sense of identity and a false sense of pressure. Pressure that we are not designed to carry.

Sometimes as Christians, we may even feel that the Bible teaches us to be perfect. For example, Matthew 5:48 says "Therefore you are to be perfect, as your Heavenly Father is perfect," but I would propose to you that we too often take that scripture out of context. So, let's take a moment to break this one down and look at it for the truth of what it is.

The word **Perfect** in the English language according to Merriam-Webster means to be without fault or defect entirely: flawless. However, when Jesus was telling us to be perfect as our Father in Heaven in perfect, this is not the definition He was using. The Hebrew word for "perfection" in Matthew 5:48 is translated as *téleios*. Téleios is known as an adjective derived from the Greek word *télos*, which is translated as a "consummated goal" or "mature. In other words, an end goal, aim, or purpose. So, in order to understand the word "perfection" in context then, we must understand that it means understanding and fulfilling a necessary process or spiritual journey, bringing something to completion.

So, you see, if we take Matthew 5:48's context into consideration we will see that perfection in our modern day understanding is not what Papa God was talking about. It is rather the pursuit of Himself, therefore obtaining maturity in character, holiness, and love, to pursue perfection in the light of who He is and who He created us to be.

> *Beloved, now we are children of God, and it has not appeared as yet what we will be. We know that when He appears, we will be like Him, because we will see Him just as He is. And everyone who has this hope fixed on Him purifies himself, just as He is pure.*
>
> I JOHN 3:2-3

We are to strive for perfection (maturity) in excellence and purification. It is the process of becoming more like Jesus and stepping more and more into His likeness and

learning how to love the way He does, unconditionally.
This is how the world will know we belong to Him - by our
love.

By this all men will know that you are My disciples, if
you have love for one another.

JOHN 13:35

I did all that I could to portray perfection by definition
of the world. I did not want to disappoint my Pawpaw or
my family, and I did not want to disappoint God. I was
afraid. I was afraid of not being wanted, loved, or
accepted. I was afraid of going to hell. However, as much
as I did not want to go to Hell, I was willing to go in
someone else's place. I remember my mom getting
frustrated with me one afternoon when I asked her if I
could take someone's place that was going to Hell. I was
not talking about anyone in particular, but I was curious if
I could take his or her place... if God would let me. I
remember saying, "If I could take their place, sending
them to Heaven, and me go to hell, I would!" I did not
understand that Jesus had already taken humanity's place
in this way and all I had to do was live in pursuit of Him,
understanding that He had already paid the price!

I just wanted to see other people whole and happy. I
wanted others to experience the God that I had seen, the
God that I knew was real and bigger than I could wrap my
little brain around. I knew there was more to Him than

what I had experienced, but I thought that I was too young to experience Him in the ways I knew others could.

Although I was taught a lot of religion - tradition, ritual, etc. - I was also taught a lot of spiritual concepts and the true reality of that realm. I came face to face with the demonic, saw demons cast out, and people set free. I understood the realness of speaking in tongues, interpretation, and the prophetic. I had conversations with demons and heard the voice of God more clearly than I can put into words, though not audibly.

Although this was what I had considered my normal, daily experienced for the majority of my life, I always believed as a child that there was much more than what I was being told or taught. My heart longed for that understanding and that relationship. I was quite confused, however, because I did not understand why I was thinking, believing, and feeling differently than what I was being told or seeing in other people's lives around me. I knew there was more depth to it but I was afraid of being wrong. So, I kept my mouth shut, my opinions to myself, and I just wondered.

My Pawpaw was just an ordinary man, yet somehow he became other people's idol - their god. He was on a throne that only God belongs on in people's hearts. Unfortunately, many in the church did not realize that this was the case. We all truly believed that we were living life the way that God intended, but living life for a man, even if he has been set up by God, is never the way to go about pursuing the heart of God. Honoring someone and setting someone up as an idol are two very different things. This is one of the reasons why learning to guard our heart and understand discernment is so crucial.

Pawpaw taught against adultery and fornication heavily, but then when I was 12 years old, he committed adultery himself, with the head deaconess of the church. I used to joke and say that our church was a cult in every way except for the lack of red Kool-Aid and literal snake handling. I remember the day I was told about witch covens in the area that were praying against our church body. These groups would get together and curse, chant, and cast spells against us. Fact is that the enemy, hell, was incredibly threatened by the power of Holy Spirit at the Church of Gainesville and did all they could to fight what Papa God was doing there. Unfortunately, the enemy took a foothold and slowly made his way into areas of Pawpaw's life and others there.

Despite all that went on in our family and church, my Pawpaw was my hero when I was a child. The church was not always bad, perverted, or wrong. My Pawpaw was an anointed man that walked in the Spirit in deep ways. I wanted to be like him - the good parts. I wanted to change people's lives but for the better. I wanted to make an impact for the good and I wanted to see heaven invade earth, even though I was oblivious as to what that meant. I wanted to see the dead raised, miracles manifest, and demons cast out. I knew all of this was possible! I wanted to be a part of change in the world and I actually wanted to do it with Papa God!

At the time, when I was much younger, I was unaware of the things that were going on behind closed doors in the church, but as I got older, things began to unfold and it caused me to question not only things about my past, but the things I believed about others, myself, and my God. What happened at the age of 8 just propelled me even deeper into these questions.

Daddy, Save Me!

"Daddy" I whispered, as I lay trapped under the back wheel of that 1970's Ford pickup truck on July 5th, 1993.
"Stay in here. If it starts to rain, hop over and roll the window up, okay?" Okay, daddy!" I replied.

He gets out of the truck, leaving the keys in the ignition. He was only going to be a couple minutes. It began sprinkling, so I hopped over in the driver seat to roll the window up. I wanted to be prepared in case it started to come down harder.

According to the police report, there was a pin that had sheared in the gear shifter causing it to fall out of park and into neutral at the slightest knock. Of course, no one was aware of the mechanical problem that was about to shift our lives, *my* life, in a big way.

I sat there playing with my little sister, Abby. She had a flare for the dramatics. She still does, which is one of the many things I love about her! I adored her giggle and often looked for ways to draw it out of her. I flung my arms back, making a gigantic "Ahhhhhhh!!!" sound, and that giggle that came from within her rang through the cab of that truck warming my heart to the deepest parts.

"Oh no!!! No! No! No! Noooo!!" I panicked.

The next thing I remember is being in the floorboard with my hands pressing against the break that conveniently decided not to work.

Black out. That couple of moments in time became lost in my memory.

And I'm back, but this time with my eye on the door and the thought running through my mind, "If I can plant my feet, maybe the truck will stop!" "I have to save Abby and Aaron!"

Without another thought in my mind, I grab hold of the door handle and swung the door open. The wind grabbed it, so I didn't have to do much pushing. With one hand I grabbed the door and with the other, the steering wheel. I looked down and planted my feet. I remember the pavement moving under my feet. It felt like every time I would touch the pavement, the truck was getting faster. It all happened so fast but so slow at the same time. I can remember the thoughts running through my mind wondering why I couldn't stop the truck and in a moment felt like a failure. I wondered if I would die. I could hear Abby screaming and in an instant realized there was nothing I could do to fix it. I look to the left and see Aaron, my 6-year-old brother, crouched down in the window. And he is gone.

Before I knew what had happened, the truck hit the curb and threw me down a 20ft embankment that was located in the middle of the city, feet from one of the busiest streets in Gainesville, GA.

I went flying through the air, landed on a stump, and continued gliding towards the bottom of the embankment. The truck followed, landing on my left ankle, running over my left thigh, and stopping ¼ inch from my head. I was trapped. Once I came to, I could hear my dad's voice. "Jesus, Jesus, Jesus, Jesus" over and over again.

Aaron had jumped from the moving truck and ran into the store where my parents were, frantically telling them that the truck was rolling down the hill. They ran out and when they did not see the truck, they ran to the edge of the parking lot only to find me lying under the 2-ton vehicle, my head just centimeters from the wheel that now had me trapped by my hair, just inches from the three feet of water sitting at the bottom of the embankment. They slid down the hill, grabbed Abby from her seat that was still secure in the cab of the truck, and they prayed while waiting on the ambulance that followed just moments later.

"Daddy" is all that I could say. I was so scared. My first thought was that I was going to be in trouble. The next was, "I do not want to go to hell. It seems a bit dramatic, but let me explain.

Getting my hair cut was not an option for me. I had been taught to believe that if I cut my hair, I would go to hell. I was terrified to get it cut. God used this incident to show me, even at that age, that my relationship with Him was not built on the length of my hair or even how perfect I could be, but simply in knowing that I belonged to Him. However, I did not feel that I could ever explain this to anyone because the way I thought and believed seemed so different from everyone else that I knew.

I wanted truth and I wanted to understand. As a child, the only thing I knew was that Papa God had kept me; He had held me in the palm of His hand. Even though I did not completely understand His tactics of protection, I knew that He was there in it all.

Fast-forwarding several years, I began to realize that like the length of my hair in determining salvation, one of the things I was taught needed to be stripped down and rebuilt. I began to understand God's grace in a whole new way on my life. Because of His goodness, He revealed so much truth to me and I began to search for real in a way I never had before.

Searching For Real Truth

At age 19 I was living with my mentor, Michelle, chasing after Papa God with everything in me. I was so hungry for love! I was exhausted by the counterfeit the world had to offer and I wanted, and needed, something real and raw. It was at this time, this age, when my world seemed to flip upside down, yet again. She taught me about the deep things of Papa God in ways that I never knew were available to me. From there, He began to show Himself in deep and beautiful ways, bringing me closer and closer to His heart.

One evening, at the age of 19, I had dinner with Pawpaw. It was the first time I had seen him in quite a while - years actually. I had distanced myself from him because I was ridiculously afraid to be anything like him and I wanted to prove to the people that had shunned me because of being his blood that I was nothing like him.

As we were sitting at dinner, the conversation escalated rather quickly. It was as if someone had taken the lid off the can of worms that had been on lockdown for so long and it stunk! The phrase that escaped his mouth caused me to almost leap over the table at him. Instead, I was met with "Honey! Kayla, please calm down!" by my great nana as I raised my hand, pointing my finger in his face with an overwhelming urge to put him in his place.

"I am the I Am," he had said incredibly confidently.

"WHAT THE HELL??!!" exploded in my mind as I felt my body give way to the force of righteous indignation. I was in serious shock. I was embarrassed for him. I was embarrassed for me. And I was angry for Papa God. How dare He put himself in that place!

We get up to walk out of the restaurant after arguing about the statement that had just been made. As we are exiting, I hear him yell at me asking how we got here. That was an easy question for me to answer!

I swing myself around still heated by the conversation we just had and out of my mouth comes:

"It's not that difficult! Satan rebelled, was cast out of Heaven with a third of the stars (or the upright ones). When we are formed in the womb, God decides which angel -

I stop. "Wait... No! That's not right!" I muttered under my breath, as I stood there utterly confused as to why in the world that just came out of my mouth.

He looks at me and begins to yell again, "YES!! Keep going! You're exactly right!!"

I just stood there watching him explain himself in total disbelief. Disbelief at what had just came out of my mouth and that he was actually defending what just came out of my mouth.

I am sure I had a look of disgust and pain in my eyes as I stood there listening to his reasoning. As angry as I was, I saw deception crawling all over him but wanted nothing to do with it. I used to feel like seeing into the spiritual was a curse, when in fact it is just the opposite. It is a blessing and one that Papa God uses to free His people. Learning how to navigate that in a Godly way took me years to figure out, and one I am still not perfect at, but He uses it and is teaching me still how to use it to pray for others, and to see others literally set free.

I stopped him.

"Pawpaw, I love you, but that is so far from the truth it's ridiculous!"

"Fine then, Kayla! If that's not it, then why don't you tell me how we got here if you're so sure!"

I was so confused. This man that knew the Word, that knew Papa God once upon a time, that raised men from the dead, cast out demons, and spoke life into people, had now committed adultery, rationalized it, believed he was I Am, and was trying to justify the fact that he believed we were stars (upright ones) cast out of Heaven and put in this mortal body to be given a second chance to go back to Heaven.

It was time for me to explain, and to be honest I was terrified. In that moment, I realized that this had been ingrained in me so deeply my whole life and I never knew it.

"We were created from dust. God created us from the dust of the earth and breathed HIS very life into us. We are a part of God but we are NOT God. Big difference! And this whole "we are stars" or "upright ones" to be given a second chance is total BS!"

As he stood there trying to feed me twisted scripture, I said that I was done, that I loved him, but that I was leaving. As I got in my car, the tears fell. What else had I believed that were lies? What else had I taken at face value just because he said it, or because my parents, friends, family or another pastor said it?

I was facing a crossroads and had a decision to make –

how was I going to approach relearning everything I ever knew? I began to truly question everything I thought to be truth and everything I thought I knew about who I was and the identity that I walked in.

These questions produced a quest for truth. I was tired of taking what others said as pure truth without checking it myself. Because Papa God had put me with Michelle, I was finally learning how to do this, how to dig my own well, how to search for myself.

Matthew 7:7-8 and Luke 11:9 both explain how if we will just pursue Him, He will show up.

Ask, and it will be given to you; seek, and you will find; knock and it will be opened to you. For everyone who asks receives, and he who seeks finds, and to him who knocks it will be opened.

MATTHEW 7:7

So I say to you, ask, and it will be given to you; seek, and you will find; knock, and it will be opened to you.

LUKE 11:9

Papa God wants to reveal Himself and the truth of who He is, the truth of heaven, and the truth of who we were created to be. We just have to take the time to ask, seek, and knock.

God, Where Were You?

That car wreck in July flooded back one afternoon while sitting in Alissa's office. I was facing this horrifying and traumatizing event for the first time in 20 years. I thought I had dealt with it, let it go, and gotten over it. I mean, I was 8 years old and within the duration of those 20 years, I should have been over it! At least that is what I told myself. Unfortunately, so many things had attached themselves to that one incident, including the time I was 19 years old realizing that so many things I had been taught had been twisted, skewed, or fell short of the fullness of truth.

"God, where were you??" I asked over and over again. I sat in Alissa's office for hours refusing to move until He answered me. I realized later that His answer was not just in regards to the wreck that happened at 8 years old, but to so many of the things in my life.

I wanted to know. I wanted to understand. I wanted to know that He had actually never left. I wanted His explanation even though He did not have to give it.

"When the bolt in the truck wiggled loose, where were You? When you knew I wasn't strong enough to push the break, where were You? When Abby started to scream, where were You? When Aaron jumped from the window, where were You? Where were You the first time my feet hit the pavement? And the second? And the third? When I laid there wondering if I was going to die, where were

You?"

These were just a few of the questions I asked. Through my tears, I continued to tell Him what He already knew..."I was so scared. I was so little. I was so weak. So, where were you? Why? Why did You let it happen? Why did You let so much in my life happen? What was the point?? I remember so much; I can still feel so much! So, what was the point? Where were You? What kind of good could possibly come out of any of this? What good could possibly come of my broken, tattered, jacked up life? Can You help me understand?"

I was so scared in the midst of so many of the things that took place in my life. I had lived in fear and now all of those feelings were back. I needed to know where He was then and I needed to know where He was as I sat in that small office reliving these events that had buried fear, hurt, and confusion in the foundation of my life. I wanted to know what I was supposed to do with it all, with the feelings. I wanted and needed His help understanding! It did not seem to add up nor did it look like it would ever help anyone else because it was not helping me.

Most often when it came to telling others about the 8 year old me that tried to stop a moving truck, I would get laughed at because people can't understand why that 8 year old little girl would risk her life like that or why she would be afraid of being in trouble. Then would come the comments of living in a cult because of the fear of getting my hair cut or the laughter towards my fear of going to hell. I felt incredibly exposed and vulnerable and it took EVERYTHING in me not to shut down!

"So," I said to Papa God, "it would be great if You could tell me where You were. Yeah, that would be great." I also asked questions of why Hell tried so desperately to end my life. "Surely hell doesn't have it out for me that much. I am just one person and not that special. So, why? Why so many deep struggles? Why so much hurt?" I explained, "You're God…You could have stopped so much! So, why make me go through so much – or allow it? Why allow so much hurt in my life, or in the life of anyone for that matter? How do I explain the why to others?? How do I understand the why myself? Going through stuff just to help someone else can't be the only answer! So, why?"

Over the years, fear had gripped my life so tightly. Fear of not being enough, fear of disappointing, of not doing anything right, and even of feeling like I should have died, that the world would have been better off without me if I had just died. The enemy swarmed my mind with so many lies throughout my life and at 8 years old, I was not equipped to deal with that attack. I did not understand that they were just lies.

During that particular session, so many big things came up. So many hurts surfaced, and I was angry at God. I was angry, but really unaware as to why, until I realized that I felt like I had been abandoned and my heart hurt for that. But even after asking all of these questions through tears, I just sat there. I sat there in silence praying that I would hear him and refusing to leave until I did. Alissa told me to sit and ask Him. To ask Him and sit there until He answered.

He answered!

"I was right there. The whole time I was right there. Baby, sometimes things happen that you don't understand but I need you to trust me. I am asking you to trust me. Trust me to hold you and keep you. Trust me to unfold it all in My time. Trust me to make sense of it in My time. Trust Me. Please.

Satan was only allowed to do so much. I did protect you. I have protected you, held you, your entire life. You were mine from the very beginning and I refused and still do refuse to ever let you go!

I want to be what defines you, what sets you apart. I was not disappointed in you and I am not disappointed in you now. I have always been right by your side because I love you. I have been here the whole time.

It is not my heart to hurt you. It is not my heart that you would hurt. I would never hurt you because you are MY child! You are Mine! I do allow things to happen but it is for a far deeper reason than you can even begin to comprehend. It is because I have a plan for you and for those that you encounter. And although you may not understand my plan, I am asking you to trust ME. I am asking you to run with Me in this life that I have given you and kept in MY grace."

I did not understand it. And to be honest, I wanted to

be angry about everything. However, I just could not remain angry anymore because I had begun to realize that although I may not always understand my circumstances, God always has a plan in the process!

Chapter Three

Running from Grace

*T*oo often we are quick to run to the wrong things or the wrong people because we do not trust or understand the power of Papa God and what He can do through our lives if we will give Him permission. He is a gentleman. He will not force Himself on us, but He will be persistent in all that He does because He loves His sons and daughters!

The church that my Pawpaw pastored split up when I was 12 years old. This man who had taught against adultery my entire life, who had loved hard and took great pride in keeping family together, succumbed to this destructive spirit himself. He began seeing a woman in our church, the head deaconess, in secret. This developed into a relationship that he had no business being in and ended with him cheating on my Nana.

When this happened, our entire family crumbled,

37

church family included. I lost everything I knew. My entire community was gone, and I lost everything that told me who I thought I was. It is hard growing up only to lose everything familiar at the age of twelve. This added a whole new dynamic to what it looked like to "find myself" and my place in the world.

A couple years after trying to find our way back to sanity, my family began going to a church close to home. I allowed "ministry" to consume all my time in a desperate attempt to find my place, purpose, and identity in the world. I pursued this for a few years, pouring myself into every bit of church that I was allowed to. I became a youth leader at fifteen. I was head of the dance team, the puppet team, worked with the children's classes, helped head up projects with the youth, and I did everything that I could to win God's approval and be worthy of the person I thought He created me to be.

Isn't that often part of the problem?

We do, do, do – performing instead of taking the time to simply accept our place with Jesus. Rather, we "work" our way into grace, trying to find ourselves when our answer simply lies within Papa God.

Learning to Sit at Papa's Feet

Mary and Martha are perfect examples of works

versus grace and why taking the time to sit at Jesus' feet is so important. Jesus makes it clear at the end of Luke 10 when He reprimands Martha and teaches her about where her priorities should lie rather than searching for approval for the things she does.

> *Now as they were traveling along, He entered a certain village; and a woman named Martha welcomed Him into her home. And she had a sister called Mary, who moreover was listening to the Lord's word, seated at His feet. But Martha was distracted with all her preparations; and she came up to Him, and said, "Lord, do You not care that my sister has left me to do all the serving alone? Then tell her to help me." But the Lord answered and said to her, "Martha, Martha, you are worried and bothered about so many things; but only a few things are necessary, really only one, for Mary has chosen the good part, which shall not be taken away from her."*
>
> LUKE 10:38-42

Papa God sees what we do, but more so, He looks at the HEART behind the things that we do. What is truly motivating us? Martha was clearly the one in the house that took charge when it came to hospitality or taking care of others. I can imagine the frustration that she felt when she was working so hard to make sure that Jesus was taken care of only to look and find Mary sitting at His feet hanging on every word that came from His mouth. Martha then proposed, pleaded with, even demanded that Jesus make Mary get up and help her. Mary understood, however, that sitting at His feet, spending time with Him, and putting herself in a position of vulnerability with Him was all that mattered. Jesus solidified this in verse 42 when He said, *"Mary has chosen the good part, which shall not be taken away from her. "*

Vulnerability is a hard word to swallow for most people. Sure, it seems to come super easy to certain fortunate people, but to others it is like swallowing a coal on fire. It is not necessarily an enjoyable experience. However, when we can let ourselves be vulnerable enough to be seen by a God that already sees us, we begin to see Him more as well.

I am guilty of struggling to be vulnerable, but I have heard it said so many times that if we want to see Him more, know Him more, and hear Him more we must actually be willing to sit at His feet and make the time and space for that, and I believe this.

For nearly 29 years of my life I was so concerned with how I made others feel, especially when it came to my relationship with Papa God, that I actually hurt any relationship I did have with Him. I had more fear of man than I had fear of Him. I was willing to please others and their wishes no matter the cost to Papa God or me. But, I choose every day to be intentional about no longer living this way.

Never Going Back

After about 2 years of pouring myself into ministry, and trying to desperately find myself, it all came to a halt when the youth pastor confronted me.

I had gone to visit my aunt and uncle's church for an Easter play one Sunday morning and when I returned on that following Tuesday night for dance class, the youth pastor asked where I had been. After telling him, he told me that if I wanted to be a youth leader, part of any other ministry at my church, I had to be there and nowhere else. Out of hurt and anger, I walked out and never returned.

I had already been wounded in the deepest of ways by church, and here it happened again. I was pouring myself out and pursuing what I thought God wanted from me, but it felt as though I was being kicked back down. Confusion hit me incredibly hard. I hated the church and everything that it seemed to stand for. I swore I would never step foot back in a church and I didn't for almost 4 years.

I refused to take part in something that was not real. I wanted real and raw. I believe that vulnerability and authenticity is something that this generation is craving and it is up to us to live our lives in such a way that vulnerability IS the normal. Where real and raw are the ordinary. Where messing up is not the end of the world, but it is something that we can be honest about while walking in forgiveness and grace.

I loved God with everything in me, but I was so angry with Him for everything that had happened in my life. I didn't know what I had done to deserve it and I felt that it was my fault. I believed the lie that I deserved it, and that I was not good enough or worth loving.

I called my mom crying and told her that I never wanted to go back to church. That if this was the way that the "church" actually was and how it treated people, if this was really how God's people are, then I wanted nothing to do with them. I began resenting and even hating Papa God to the point of nearly throwing my life away.

I was once again swimming in a pool of victimization. I felt sorry for myself. Not only was I angry with God and myself but I was angry with my family. I was angry that I had been given the Buckner name and that the Buckner blood flowed through my veins. I was embarrassed, hurt, angry, bitter, and I let this all take hold of my heart, even though it hurt.

Isn't it amazing how anger and bitterness
can be so incredibly damaging?
It can destroy who you are and control the
choices you make.
Yet when it comes to letting it go, we struggle because
the convenience and the comfort of the uncomfortable is
far greater than the desire to let it go.

Cliff Diving

At 16 years old I quit church, began doing drugs, and became addicted very quickly. I started with smoking marijuana and that quickly escalated to snorting lines of anything I could get my hands on. The things I did within that first month alone should have killed me or put me in jail. By the end of that month I had done countless drugs, began partying every night, and began sleeping around.

The drugs numbed my feelings, the alcohol helped me express myself in ways I would not have otherwise, and sleeping with men put me in control. I hated men and I wanted control rather than being controlled. I would use them because I wanted to feel something, anything besides hate for myself. But the drugs, alcohol and sex, among other things, just made it all worse.

Papa God refused, however, to leave me alone, and it pissed me off. He tried so many times to get my attention. I would have dreams, visions, and hear Him talk to me louder than I ever had. So, I would do more drugs to try and drown Him out. I thought that maybe if I did enough crank, smoked enough weed, or had enough sex that He would leave. I hated Him. But He never left.

I did not understand His love for me. It seemed too good to be true. It eventually scared the hell out of me – literally. His pursuit of us is not a game, it is not fake, and He is relentless.

*You have enclosed me behind and before, and laid Your
hand upon me. Such knowledge is too wonderful for me;
it is too high, I cannot attain to it. Where can I go from
your spirit? Or where can I flee from Your presence? If I
ascend to heaven, You are there; if I make my bed in
Sheol, behold, You are there. If I take the wings of the
dawn, if I dwell in the remotest part of the sea, even
there Your hand will lead me, and You right hand will
lay hold of me.*

PSALM 139:5-12

Attempted Escape

How often do we run out of fear of being known, truly
known? Drugs, alcohol, and sex were my escape. They
were my escape from what I thought was reality.
Unfortunately, this is not just my story. I have
encountered so many people who have turned to drugs,
alcohol, sex, partying, books, puzzles, work – pretty much
anything to drown out their pain and hurts.

I want to back up just a little and tell you the story
about a night that changed my life forever. The drugs
started the night of May 1st, 2002. It was the beginning of
my forever and I was headed straight for Hell.

I found out that night that a friend had been lying to
me for nearly a year about doing drugs. She was the one
person I thought I could trust. I put my whole heart into
our friendship. I remember thinking so many times during

44

that year that I finally had someone I could count on, someone who got me, someone who actually just loved me for me. I was sadly mistaken and I felt betrayed.

"Pinky promise me that you won't tell a soul! If you do, Kayla, I swear to God that I will deny it and our friendship is over!" she said.

"Okay." I said a bit nervous and apprehensive, but my curiosity won the agreement.

I sat in the front seat of that black Monte Carlo with my knees pulled to my chest as she unloaded her secret. I sat there staring out the window looking at the field we were passing by as everything inside of me became numb. I felt like everything inside of me was crumbling and I did not know how to make it stop. Once more, I was made a fool. I was lied to, and taken advantage of. I was a joke. My heart broke a little more that night.

"Why is this happening?" This thought ran through my mind as I sat there sinking a little more inside myself. I tried being that perfect friend but instead became a cover up for what truly was rather than being loved just because.

"You know that saying keep your friends close and your enemies closer?" she asked. "Well…"

I cannot quite put into words what all happened to me that night except that Hell got its way. I caved. I gave in. I wanted to give up, so I did.

"What can you get and can you get it tonight?" I asked.

Seriously confused and a little taken back, she looks at me shocked and says, "ummm... I can get some weed, and yeah, I can get it tonight! Wait... Are you being serious!?"

I looked at her with a determination that I had never felt before and responded with "Hell yes! I'm serious!"

I called my dad and asked if I could stay out a little later. I was a "good kid" so he had no reason to suspect anything and off we went. My life dramatically shifted that night. I got high for the first time. I experienced tears, a hardened heart, and my entire circle of friends finally being honest with me. I hated my life. I hated who I was! I hated who I thought I was created to be and I was not prepared or willing to learn who I truly was!

Quick Defiance

One high led to the next. I was still feeling too much and I wanted out. I wanted out of this shell of a life. Chasing one high to the next became my daily goal. I was trying to escape from all of the hurt that was on its way to catch up with me. Little by little it was all becoming too much and I did not understand why I was not strong enough to fight it, to stand up to what I knew with all of my heart was nothing more or less than a spiritual battle. I knew that hell was after me but I became weary and stopped caring if it was.

I was afraid of where I was headed but I continued going deeper; I chose to go deeper. I continued to run from God because I was angry, bitter, and I had so much unforgiveness in my heart. I did not feel worthy of Him or His love. I thought He was mad at me, and rightfully so, but then on the other hand, I was just angrier with myself because I felt like I had failed. I failed myself and I failed Him. So, running harder and faster I did.

Running faster and harder brought me face to face with death in a very real way. One night in the middle of April while sitting in my boyfriend's truck in my dad's driveway, I came to understand the reality of life and death in a way I had not experienced before.

I had become friends with huffing. It became a new fascination because when I would do it, I thought I sounded like Cher. If you can picture this, I was standing on the front porch of a double wide trailer hiding on acres and acres of land in the middle of the Northeast Georgia mountains belting out "Do you believe in life after love" at the top of my lungs (or what was left of them after inhaling deadly chemicals that should have ripped my insides to shreds). As funny as the singing may seem, what happened next is far from humorous.

I sat inside of this truck that particular night holding what almost took my life. I remember looking at the fluorescent blinking clock that taunted me as I sat there waiting for the high to wear off. 12:31 am it read. The "high" was only supposed to last about 10 seconds. I sat there laughing for a moment until that 10 seconds turned into much more. My breathing became more shallow and thoughts raced through my mind, crashing one by one, hitting me like ton of bricks. "What is wrong? Why am I not coming down?? I don't understand!"

My boyfriend just sat there unaware of what was happening. I begin asking through tears, "What am I doing with my life? Why am I doing this? I don't actually want to die. I can't die. I know that if I die right now, I will go to hell. I have so many things I want to do. Why am I hurting so bad? Why can't I just be okay? I hate my life but I don't want to die!" Fear began to grip my heart even tighter.

As fast towards Hell as I was running, the reality of it being so close scared me intensely. "I can't do this!" I cried. I look up and over at the time. 12:34 am. I begin to panic even more. Something was not right. Something did not feel right. I could feel my life coming to an end, literally feeling myself slip away. I look out into the darkness of the woods through the windshield. I begin to see darkness close in around me. I knew this may be it and I was acutely aware of the consequence I was faced with in that very moment.

I was about to die.

"God! If you will let me live, I promise I will never touch this stuff again! Please don't let me die yet. I'm not ready!" I pleaded as tears ran down my face understanding the reality of what was coming for me.

Not a moment went by and the high was gone like I

had never even touched it before. I look down and the catalyst of this high laid in my lap. I picked it up and threw it across the truck and told my boyfriend to get rid of it. I wanted nothing to do with it, I did not want it around me, and I did not want it anywhere around my family. I knew in that moment that whether I liked it or not, Papa God had me and He was not going anywhere. One incredibly beautiful thing about God is that even when we give up, He does not. His pursuit of me became even more relentless.

Because of His love for us, He refuses to let us go. Ephesians 1:4 says "just as He chose us in Him before the foundations of the world, that we would be holy and blameless before Him. In love He predestined us to adoption as sons through Jesus Christ Himself, according to the kind intention of His will..."

According to this scripture, He marked us before we were even conceived. There is nothing that I could have ever done in my past and there is nothing that I could ever do in the future to make Him love me any less or any more. It is by His grace, and His grace alone, that we are set free.

"In Him we have redemption through His blood, the forgiveness of our trespasses according to the riches of His grace."

EPHESIANS 1:7

I tried running from grace, from Papa God, but He was going nowhere fast! His pursuit for your heart is literally so relentless that He would go to the cross over and over again just to hold you. I tried shutting Him out, ignoring Him, and I tried holding on to control, but that did nothing but shove me deeper into a very dark hole that was lonely and depressing.

When we come to a place of surrender, that is when we begin to see things for what they really are. It is there that the darkness is brought to light. The enemy is just that - your enemy. Hell is not your friend! Hell does not want the best for you and all of these "temporary fixes" are just that; They are temporary and they are not going to last. They are not eternal! Papa God promises – HE PROMISES – eternal life and life more abundantly WITH Him if we will just lay our lives down, surrender, and trust that He is who He says He is.

It *is* possible to live in divine encounter, to experience Him fully at all times. It is not a fantasy. In fact, living life with Him is more real than what we know to be reality. It is not magical or mystical. It is truth and it is beautiful!

Are you willing to surrender your
temporary for His eternal??

Chapter Four

Searching for Freedom

O ne of the things that I realized in my late 20s is that I had lived for so long at the mercy of what others wanted, being what they wanted me to be rather than who I was created to be. My life was all about making others happy at my own expense, even though I had convinced myself that I was happy no matter what life looked like. Isn't it ironic how we can live so selfishly and independently for our own hearts and desires, but at the same time demand others to make us happy? We lay out impossible standards and expectations for others regarding our own happiness and it produces deep spaces in our hearts where bitterness and hurt are born.

I lived in such a way to where what other people did in my life dictated my happiness, my joy, and my freedom. I did not do this on purpose, but the desire to please others over Papa God snuck in at a very young age and it became my normal. I wanted so badly to be loved that I could not help but cater to others, regardless of the repercussions in my own life.

I had to fight to get to a place of freedom. It was an intentional decision; it required determination to be joyful and walk in that regardless of my situation or circumstances. I had to fight to overcome the desire to please man or let others decide how I lived my life, and learned to rely only on Papa God for my freedom. True freedom only comes from Him! He makes this very clear in John 8:34-36 –

"Jesus answered them, "Truly, truly I say to you, everyone who commits sin is the slave of sin. The slave does not remain in the house forever; the son does remain forever. So, if the Son makes you free, you will be free indeed.""

When we rely on others besides Papa God for our happiness, joy, and freedom, we are misplacing an emotional dependency that only belongs to Papa God. This dependency can actually bind both us and those we chose to depend on by holding them to expectations they are simple unable to fulfill. This is when unhealthy relationships are formed, and the reality of co-dependent relationships means that Papa God has very little room to do what He wants with you, individually and/or relationally.

For a time, my happiness depended on whether or not someone wanted to do something with me, how someone looked at me, whether or not someone would contact me first, or if someone would tell me they loved me. I was relying solely on others for affirmation and not on Papa God Himself. Truthfully, my wavering happiness hinged on the fact that I didn't feel worthy enough to be loved by others, even though I was told over and over again that I was loved and worthy of love. My mind continued to cling on to the lies of the enemy. Unfortunately, I had adopted the mentality of being worthless and unlovable as a lifestyle

I longed for freedom during that time but I did not know how to get it. I was comfortable with the chains of acceptance, and the familiar kept me bound, it was what I knew best. The pursuit of acceptance seemed easier than it would have been to pursue the heart of Papa God. The enemy had me convinced that if I pursued Jesus, I would lose everything else. He was half right.

I did lose many people in my life. I had to lay my life on the alter. I had to walk away from what I knew, my comforts, and my false security in pursuing everyone else but the One I should have been pursuing from the beginning. I had to surrender my control, but I gained everything in the process!

Seventeen Candles

At the age of 17 my world crumbled under my feet and I was anything but okay. I did learn, however, that it is okay to not be okay, as long as you don't stay there. You were created for far more than to remain broken, lost, and lonely.

That October, we got the news that my uncle had committed suicide. To be completely honest, I questioned if this was real; I did not believe that there was any way that he could have taken his own life. On the other hand, because of where my life has been, there *have* been times that I could understand why he would want to take his own life.

About a month after my uncle chose to leave this world, and right before Thanksgiving, the same man that tinted my innocence as a little girl, attempted to rape me again. My mom ran into him a few months earlier and because we had not seen him in years, he asked us over for dinner. I did not understand why my parents agreed, but as a family we went.

I still saw this man as my "uncle," so even though I did not understand why we were going, part of me was excited. However, I also carried with me an anxious feeling that was quite confusing. We visited a few times for dinner after that, a couple of those times of which I showed up high on some type of drug. I could not explain what I felt when I had to go over there, but I did whatever

I could to mask what I was feeling.

After visiting a few times for dinner, he asked my mom to have me come over to stay the night and help with his two foster kids because their third foster child needed tubes put in her ears. So I went to help feed the kids dinner and get them to bed. Later that night I was sitting on the couch when he came over and sat on the opposite side across from me, grabbing my foot to rub it.

As a little girl, I used to throw my feet in people's faces wanting for someone to rub them, so, call me naïve, but when this happened I honestly did not think much of it. Instead, we sat there and had a long conversation about the past and how the church had been before, and he shared with me his thoughts on the things that happened.

Afterwards, I felt as though I should have known better. After all, he did cheat on his incredible wife years earlier with a young girl, who was just seventeen years old. I always believed the best about people, however, and I let my guard down.

He got up to go to bed, turned off all the lights, walked by and smacked me on the butt. I felt a bit awkward but I didn't say anything because I was confused by what had just happened. He followed up with, "if you get cold, you can come crawl in the bed with me." "I'll be okay" I replied as I clutched a bit tighter to the pillow I was hugging, a bit weirded out.

What would happen hours later haunted my memories for the next 13 years.

I was coming to, struggling to understand what was happening to me, what was pulling me out of my sleep. The sun had not yet begun to show it's face and I could hear faint music drifting from the direction of the television. Then suddenly everything snapped clear. My eyes were open and all I could see was his face inches from my own. Fear shot through my body as I realized his right hand was in my pants. As I struggled to get away, he tried desperately to get my pants off, ripping them, as I broke free.

I leaped over the coffee table creating a barricade between him and I. The adrenaline pumping through my body caused me to tremble as I stood there yelling and cursing through my tears at the betrayal. And he just sat there. With his arms propped up on the back of the couch and a smirk that reached from one side of his face to the other, he was telling me that he knew he had won.

"You might as well just keep your mouth shut. No one will believe you, and if they do, you know you wanted it. No one will do anything about it anyways," he said.

I fought to conceal the fear racing through my body, but the trembling told a different story. After standing there for just a moment trying desperately to make sense of what had just happened, my thoughts turned to the kids. What about them? What horrific things had they experienced at the hands of this man? I had to keep them safe. Somehow it felt like my responsibility. I knew what this man was capable of and it scared me. It sickened me.

I took a deep breath and got the kids ready for school and on the bus. I was getting into my car when he leaped off the front porch grabbing the door of my car door before I could get away. He proceeded to tell me what I always meant to him. How I was always his favorite and how I always had a special place in his heart. We stood there arguing as I dreaded the idea of what could happen. He was much stronger than I was.

It was not but just a moment when he began talking about that precious two year old they had at the hospital. I became sick. This was no longer about me, but about that innocent little girl.

"You two share the same place in my heart now. She reminds me of you when you were little. She loves me and I love her, the same way I love you," he said proudly.

I wanted to throw up. It was all I could do to hold myself together. All I could manage to say was how disgusting he was and that he wouldn't get away with it. He found that quite hilarious.

I got in my car as he tried to kiss me. I shoved him away, closed my door, and locked it as fast I possibly could.

"School. I just have to get to the school. He can't do anything to me there." I recited over and over again in my mind on the way to my high school that morning. I do not remember the drive, but I do remember tears falling. I did not know what to do. I was in shock.

I sat there on the cold floor in the hallway of my

school, heart heavy, and my mind reeling from the things that were said right before I left.

"How in hell could a man hurt such a small, helpless little girl??" I asked myself. I had not yet remembered the things that had happened when I was little so the power of the feelings I was experiencing did not make sense. I wanted to disappear. I wanted to hide and never be found again. I had, yet again, been taken advantage of, hurt, and abused and I did not understand why. "What had I done?" became a common question in my mind.

My best friend at the time walked in smiling and laughing as always, but when she saw me, she immediately noticed something was off. I could not talk. I could not do much of anything. I remember looking at her with a blank stare, tears falling down my cheeks. I could not form words. I was so scared. She asked what was wrong and wanted to know why I looked white as a ghost. Because I could not talk, and because writing was my go-to way of processing, I sat in first period and wrote her a letter giving a description of what happened. The silence did not last long before she burst into my second period class and pulled me out into the hallway.

"Kayla! You have to tell your parents!"

"You don't understand! You don't know who this man is. Even *if* I told them, it's not like they would believe me." I told her as I stood there shaking. I was slightly afraid that he would show his face in my school. I did not feel safe anywhere. After arguing with her for a while, I finally agreed to tell my parents when she said that if I didn't tell them, she would.

Later that evening, I went into my parent's room, sat down on the edge of their bed and through gritted teeth and tears, I told them what happened. My dad was turning red and I remember he and my mom just looking at one another. I sat there wondering what was going to happen as my dad went off talking about all the things he *wanted* to do... but somehow we all knew that nothing would be done.

My mom looked at me and with a strange look in her eyes says, "I knew that was going to happen." Then she got up, went in her bathroom, and started cleaning. That was it.

I sat there wondering what had just happened. I did not understand why they had given me that response. To be honest, I was not all that surprised, but I suppose I was hoping for something different.

More often than not, there is a lot more going on under the surface than we see. There is often something going on that we may either miss or not understand. When it came to my mom, there were things that she had been through in the past, things she herself had buried, things that I was unaware of and when this situation happened with me, the easiest thing for her was to almost dismiss it at the time – a learned coping mechanism.

Being reminded of our past is not always fun but sometimes it is necessary for healing.

I went to bed and cried myself to sleep. The next day at school, mom showed up at my high school and took me to the sheriff's office. I had to tell everything again…three times. After going through all of this, my parents dropped the charges. When I asked why, they said they did not want me going through the process that was inevitably coming if they proceeded. From my viewpoint, I was already going through it, and I wanted him to pay. The one good thing that came from it was that the kids were removed from his care. He would never be able to hurt them. That was worth my pain.

About two weeks after this happened my mom told me that she was leaving my dad. What happened to me was the "straw that broke the camel's back" she said. There was a lot going on in my parent's relationship apart from me, but the timing of this made me feel that it was my fault. Although I did not ask for any of this to happen, it did, and this was just part of the repercussion of what the enemy was doing.

When my mom left and took my sister with her, I followed her for a short time, while my brother chose to stay with my dad. I moved out soon after however because in March of that year she accused me of knowing that a "friend" stole money from her. For about 5 months I floated around with nowhere to live. I had been working two jobs at this time but I could not afford my own place. I bounced around from friend to friend, sleeping in cars, on cots, couches, or wherever I could land.

I was so confused.
I was so hurt.
I was so angry.
I continued to run away from Papa God.
I did not understand why the enemy was so
relentless in the pursuit of my life. I did not understand
why hell was after my very life.
I wanted nothing more than to die!

After all that had happened that year and I blew out
my hypothetical seventeen candles, I did not believe that I
could survive much more. I wondered where God was. I
wondered what I had done to deserve all of these things.
Aside from a couple of years as a teenager, I was a good
kid. My heart was all for Papa God and loving people. I
wanted to know Jesus but I did not know how to do that
and I was literally grasping onto anything that I could that
would help me escape this Hell I had found myself in.

Hanging On By A Thread

Sitting in Alissa's office, I sat staring at the wall this time.

I thought I was fine, but the tears streaming down my
face and the involuntary shaking I was experiencing
obviously said otherwise.

It had been almost 13 years since I last really looked at
this for what it was. Some called me a liar, some called me

dirty, and others called me damaged goods, among other horrible labels given. I believed every last word and it dictated in an even deeper way how I lived my life every day thereafter.

The truth was that the people who had said these horrible things about me had no idea about the past that I had endured before this night happened. No one would have wanted me at all had they known what had really taken place as I was growing up, which is why I kept quiet and tried just catering to other's wants.

I was sitting in Alissa's office and we were almost done. I thought maybe just seeing her a couple more times would do it; I would tie up the loose ends and solidify the fact that I had made it through Hell and back, and I would be back to me for good. That's what I thought.

I sat there on the white couch that had become my safe place. It was where I sat every week while I met with her, ready for whatever she would throw at me, or ready for whatever Papa had for me in that time. I came to the realization that Papa God operates in His own perfect timing and this day was no different.

Sitting there on that particular day she asked me to go back to 13 years (nearly one month after my parents separated and headed toward divorce) and just dive in to see if anything came up with this particular incident that I swore I was "over." To me, feeling I was "over it" made sense because I didn't feel anything anymore when I was asked about that time. I was so very wrong. I may have learned how to cope and shut down the memories and emotions by burying them deep, but I had not dealt with them at all.

As I closed my eyes, I was back in that place. Back in that dark and empty living room. Music blaring, lights off, colored strobe lights piercing through the darkness, a couch, and a lot of alcohol. And just down the hall was a room that would become my own personal jail cell, my Hell on earth.

I was running so hard and so fast from everything and everyone. I was angry with God because of life happening. I was mad. I was hurt. And I wanted nothing to do with God so I did everything in my power to drown Him out and alcohol was all I could get my hands on this night.

The guys I was with, Jake and Ethan, kept feeding me drinks and one after another I took them down. I just wanted to forget and I wanted to remember. I wanted to remember and I wanted to forget. I wanted to feel and I wanted to numb out. I just wanted out. I couldn't get out of my own head. So, one drink after another and down they went. Down I went.

Down I went back to the bathroom that was no more than 20 feet from where I had started. I felt horrible, but at least I was feeling something. I felt so much that I became even more numb. I don't know if I was given something else other than alcohol, but at that point it didn't seem to matter.

I was in the bathroom propped up against the toilet for

what seemed like forever. There were only three of us at the house that night. Jake and Ethan were both supposed to be my friends. I was so adamant to Jake before we came to watch out for me. If I was so worried about it, why did I go in the first place? I have asked myself that question so many times. Truth is that I sincerely thought I would be protected and I just wanted an escape from reality for a while and free alcohol was the way to my destination of nothingness, even if just for a short time.

I became so fatigued sitting up against the toilet that I could barely hold myself up anymore. I just wanted to lie down. Something wasn't right. I had been drunk several times before but this was different. I felt different. I was so drunk but I remember everything from that night. I remember laughing. I remember being angry. I remember throwing back more shots because the one before wasn't doing its job quick enough. I just needed it to do its job quicker.

Jake came to the bathroom and asked me if I wanted him to try to take me the 20 feet back to the couch in the living room or if I wanted to crawl to the bed that was five feet away. I opted for the bed because it was closer. He helped me up and left me there with a trashcan beside my head.

I laid there looking down the hall. Music still blaring so loud you couldn't hardly hear yourself think. I saw someone coming. Hoping that it was nothing, I closed my eyes for just a moment.

I heard the door lock. Why did I hear the door lock?

Before I knew it, Ethan was on top of me, begging me to give him what he wanted. When I refused, his begging became demand. My no was no match for his desire to take what he wanted and I was too weak to fight him off. As the wrestling progressed and the demand became fiercer, so did his strength. I wanted to get away, tried to get away even, but I was no match for him. I hoped that Jake would hear me yelling no repeatedly and come and protect me, but he didn't show.

What was I supposed to do? It was my fault after all, I thought, and had I not been drunk, this would have never happened. Unfortunately, these are the thoughts that flood the minds of the girls and guys that this happens to far too often. This is a lie from hell! It does not matter the situation or circumstance of what happened to you! You did not deserve being taken advantage of, violated, or hurt!

With tears streaming down my face, a pleading in my voice, and weakness in my body, Ethan grabbed ahold of my waist and flips me to my stomach. I tried to get away, but I soon passed out from the pain. I woke up the next morning hurting physically and angry that I, once more, was not only taken advantage of, but also left unprotected by the one person who was supposed to have my back.

After gathering myself, I found my clothes and headed towards the living room where Jake was. He was lying on the couch and as he begrudgingly stared at me, I asked why he didn't come.

"It sounded like you wanted it, Kayla!" he defended.

Although I was pleading with Ethan to stop, Jake felt as though it was not enough to warrant his help and I was left for someone to have their way with me, again.

All of this floods back into my memory sitting on that white couch. I have dealt with so much over the past year and a half at this point – remembering, processing, remembering, processing, rinse and repeat over and over and over again. I honestly thought that this was just a distant memory. But I was horribly mistaken.

I open my eyes and as the tears reemerged, I look at Alissa. All I could get out was how I didn't understand where this was coming from and that "I should be over it." A couple minutes go by and all I could manage to do was sit and stare at the wall.

My heart raced as I asked Papa why it was that thirteen years later this was still hurting so bad. My emotions were getting the best of me and I tried to hold it together but the more I tried to hold it together, the harder it was for me to do so.

I was so gently reminded that I have been given beauty for ashes, joy for mourning, and that everything that was taken from me, including my innocence as a child, would be given back. I used to believe that I was nothing. I used to believe that I was worthless, trash, tainted, unworthy, unwanted, despised, rejected, hated, ugly, damaged goods, and completely unlovable, but I know better now. I know better now because my Jesus says otherwise.

> *For you formed my inward parts; you knitted me together in my mother's womb. I praise you, for I am fearfully and wonderfully made. Wonderful are your works; my soul knows it very well. My frame was not hidden from you, when I was being made in secret, intricately woven in the depths of the earth. Your eyes saw my unformed substance; in your book were written, every one of them, the days that were formed for me, when as yet there was none of them.*
>
> PSALM 139:13-16

This scripture alone tells us of our worth to Him. However, as true as this is and as loud as it screams unconditional love, I let the enemy talk me into believing the complete opposite. My heart was so hurt that I believed that I was every bit of worthless, damaged goods, trash, and unlovable. This was the catalyst to me shutting down.

Fighting Freedom

I often wondered if I would actually ever walk in freedom. Shutting down, for so many years was my own kind of freedom. It was the easy way out. However, my way out just held me hostage.

Shutting down, closing off, and building walls is

dangerous and the enemy knows this. Doing this does not guard your heart, nor will it keep you from getting hurt or from facing disappointment. Not only does it create boundaries between you, other people, and God, but it also keeps you bound. It paves the road to being a victim rather than an overcomer.

Although there are times for it, our hearts were not created for solitude. We were created for relationship with others and with Jesus. We were created for community. Hear me when I say that there are times for alone time with Father God, but we were very much created for fellowship. Galatians 6:2, for instance, says to "bear one another's burdens, and so fulfill the law of Christ." Later, the author in Hebrews 10 explains how we are to encourage one another in such a way that we fight for freedom together.

> *"and let us consider how to stimulate one another to love and good deeds, not forsaking our own assembling together, as is the habit of some, but encouraging one another, and all the more as you see the day drawing near."*
>
> HEBREWS 10:24-25

When we go through these things, we do not have to have it all together! It is okay to not always be okay. Papa God will hold you together in your brokenness and in your unraveling. He will place others in your life at times to walk through the hurts, pain, and joy with you. There will be times when stuff comes up, and times when we have to face the things that have happened to us, whether it was twenty years ago, five years ago, or right now in this moment.

This is because we have a Father that loves us that much!

He refuses to let us stay buried in our past or pain. He is strategic in His timing in peeling back the layers because He knows exactly when and what we can and cannot handle. The beautiful part is that if we let Him, He will use our struggles, pain, mess-ups, successes, highs, and lows to show His nature and raw love to others, change their hearts and lives, and in turn change the world.

Chapter Five

Let's Talk About Sex

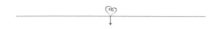

I became numb. Shades of color hit the light differently and became skewed. Smells were no longer as powerful. Taste became bland. I had lost myself. Let's be real...I never really knew who I was to begin with. I became someone I was never created to be in the first place.

Homosexuality is not something that I wrestle with... anymore.

I recognize, realize rather, that some may not understand or like what I'm about to share, but that is okay. I realize that this may be hard for others to swallow, but that too is okay. This is part of my story. This is a drop of the life I lived. A glimpse of who I thought I was, not

71

who I actually am.

Homosexuality was something that I wrestled with for a lot longer than I have wanted to admit, and it wasn't just a college experience. So many of my friends that I had in and out of college liked to justify their experiences and choices as part of a normal and experimental college phase. Because of this, they like to reassure themselves the things I experienced were just that, a college experience.

Many of the people who did know about my experience with homosexuality never really knew about my childhood, and if they did, they most often dismissed it like yesterday's garbage. This was not necessarily a bad thing, however, dismissing the struggles, the abuse, and the pain from my past did not give me the room to face those things and heal properly. But, I did the same. I did not give myself permission to face my past for a long time.

When I say I wrestled with homosexuality, I mean that I did not want to be gay but I very much believed that I was. Hell was fighting me, wrestling me, breathing lies in my ears, and rather than letting Papa God fight my battle for me, I thought I could do it on my own. I was Miss. Independent. I was capable of doing it on my own! Or so I thought.

Our struggle is not against flesh and blood but against principalities, powers and the rulers of darkness in high places.

EPHESIANS 6:10-13

Believing this lie, that I was someone that I was not created to be, wore me down. I was already tired of fighting and I let Satan talk me into believing the lie that I was in fact gay. However, truth trumps fact and the truth was that I was created a daughter, royalty, wanted, chosen, whole, and pure in every way. Truth was that I was not created to live in perversion. The truth was that my identity was not wrapped up in homosexuality even though I believed it was.

The Word talks about homosexuality in several places. Unfortunately, we often like to focus just on the laws in Leviticus or of the sins in Sodom and Gomorra. In fact, homosexuality is mentioned in other places such as Romans 1:26, 1 Corinthians 6:9, and 1 Timothy 1:8-10. We could get into a bunch of antics and tear these scriptures apart, but rather than doing that, I want to talk about Jesus and His heart on the matter.

Jesus never mentioned homosexuality on its own, He did however mention sexual immorality. The Greek translation for sexual immorality in the New Testament is often translated as *porneia,* which is also translated into fornication or idolatry. If we break this down even further, we will find that this is a form of surrendering sexual purity.

Flee immorality. Every other sin that a man commits is outside the body, but the immoral man sins against his own body.

1 CORINTHIANS 6:18

Lets establish one basic truth: God designed sexuality and He designed it as a pure and beautiful thing. The Bible makes it clear in Matthew 19 that a man is to leave his father and mother and be joined to his wife, as one flesh. This shows us that marriage and sex was created for one man and one woman within the confines of marriage and anything outside of this is abusing the beautiful gift that was given to us. This includes much more than just homosexuality but sexual immorality in general!

The Word is clear about this in the New Testament when 1 Corinthians 6:9 tells us, "or do you not know that the unrighteousness will not inherit the kingdom of God? Do not be deceived; neither fornicators (*those that have sex outside of marriage, including adultery*), nor idolaters (*worshiping or giving excessive devotion to something or someone other than Father God – putting anything above Him*), nor adulterers (*sex between a married person and someone who is not their spouse*), nor effeminate (*basically living a lifestyle that is opposite of a person's God-given gender*), nor homosexuals (*someone attracted to or engaging in sex with someone of their same gender*), nor thieves (*a person who steals another person's property*), nor the covetous (*desiring something that someone else*

74

possesses), nor drunkards (*someone who is frequently and obsessively drunk*), nor revilers (*someone who uses abusive or/mocking and disrespectful language against someone else*), nor swindlers (*someone who cheats or scams other people for money*), will inherit the kingdom of God.

If we will pay attention to this, we will notice that someone who commits adultery, steals, or is a drunkard is in just as much sin as someone who is living a homosexual lifestyle. So then, why do we dismiss this truth? How often do we look past these other things because we would not say that we are fornicators, adulterers, thieves, drunks, or even covet someone or something. We do not have any issues seeing these other things as sin but when it comes to homosexuality, we often dismiss it as if it was a mistake that it was written in the Word at all. As if God, or the writer that was inspired by God Himself, heard Him wrong on this one issue.

The truth is that God does not change, His character does not change, and what He has established as wrong and right does not change just because our culture or society changes. He does not change His mind just because culture is uncomfortable with facing truth. He does not change who He is because culture does not like to admit they are wrong. However, just because He does not change His mind and His Word does not change does not mean that His love is any less than when He formed you in the womb and called you unto Himself!

Even though I knew that living this way was wrong, living this lifestyle was the only thing that made sense at the time, especially according to how I lived my life. It was a place I felt I belonged. I had searched for so long to feel something other than abandoned, unwanted, and dismissed that I took what I could get. The community took me in and treated me like one of their own. I wanted to feel loved and wanted and they did just that. I wanted to belong. I longed to belong. But this love that I thought I was receiving was a counterfeit love. The enemy worked overtime to make sure they held me and made it seems impossible to get loose.

There were times that I beat myself up, wondering why it was something that was part of my life at all. "Why couldn't it just go away?" was a frequent question I asked because despite my feelings I knew it was wrong. It was not just something that I have read in the Word or something that I have been told was wrong, but I knew in my heart that this is not how I was designed to live nor did it have a place in what I was created for. But, even though I asked the question, I wasn't willing to give it up most of the time because it occupied a space that was empty. It became comfortable and how I defined myself. I had found my identity in that.

But, that was the answer to my question of why - why homosexuality was something that was part of my life and why it wouldn't just go away.
I wasn't willing to let it go.

Giving that all up, letting go of the identity I had become so familiar with meant that I would have to face myself, my true self, and I did not know who that girl was. I was afraid of what I might find. I was convinced that it was too hard and that I was not strong enough. In and of myself I was not, but I was not willing to give it up. I did not desire freedom more than the comfort of counterfeit love and acceptance.

Isn't it interesting how the enemy will try to convince you of your identity, talk you into believing a lie, and then shame you and drown you in fear? Isn't it interesting how the enemy wants nothing more than to destroy you and your destiny? That is because he understands that if you get ahold of who you truly are, and understand your identity lies in Papa God, you will ruin Hell and destroy Satan's plans for you.

Hiding in Plain Site

I used to go about my days as if everything was normal, as if I was happy. I walked around with a permanent mask that hid my pain underneath, and I was good at hiding. It was easier to bury my emotions than it was to face them.

Hiding became my coping mechanism. It was safer to hide than it was to be vulnerable and risk being hurt even more, even deeper. I went through several times in my life where my emotions would literally get the best of me. I would cry at the drop of a hat and it seemed like anything that was said or done to me would flip a switch. It was like pulling a trigger on a shotgun. It would hit my heart, spark an old memory or emotion, and then I would lose control. It eventually sent me in a tailspin of depression and bondage. I was drowning in my own pool of victimization and I was completely clueless as to how to escape.

I did a good job at lying for a long time, at least I thought that I did. I also did a good job at keeping a secret, or at least I thought that I did. The truth is I was living a lie; I was not living in freedom in the least bit. I was actually dying slowly inside. I was locked up. I was held captive. I was held prisoner in my own body and mind.

I am not proud of the secrets, the lies, or the blatant slap in Papa God's face that I gave over, and over, and over again. But the secrets were not what was killing me, it was all the things that led up to my secrets. It was all the hurt and the lies that had been burning inside of me for so long that kept me locked up. It was the confusion of my past and not understanding why I couldn't remember part of it that held me captive for so long. It was the abuse, the lies that I was not good enough, the shame and insecurities, and the belief that I was not worthy of love that held me prisoner.

Writing this book is not easy for me! In fact, I have fought sharing my story for some time because, to be quite honest, I have feared a lot that may come with it. I was buried in shame for so long! I have feared that some would walk away. I have feared being seen differently; I have feared that others would see me in the darkness of my past rather than the light of who I am now – simply a daughter of the King and a lover of Jesus! I want to be seen not in light of my past but as a girl that has been set free - free from far more than just sexual impurity.

Let me be clear – when I say sexual impurity, I mean just that. Whether that is living with someone outside of marriage, sleeping around, or messing around with someone that is not your spouse, it is all impurity, and they are all things I have done.

I have feared family or friends being disappointed. I have feared being misunderstood. I have feared being mocked or made fun of. I have feared being torn down or shamed. I have feared losing people, and being left. I have feared that those that are living this lifestyle would feel that I was judging them (which is not at all the case). It is not my heart to judge or condemn anyone! Rather, I have walked in fear and shame from these things in my life that nearly killed me, and I refuse to live there any longer! I will not let fear or shame beat me!

Hurt People Hurt People

My life was not my own for the simple fact that I gave myself away to others. For a long time I gave my life to so many other people except to the One I should have handed it over to permanently. And I don't think I was alone in this. So many of us tend to look to others for our identity when we don't truly understand who we are, don't we?

But why do we do this? It is a question I have asked myself over and over again, but for me it has not gone unanswered.

The truth? I saw myself as less. Like so many others, I have been hurt and abused over and over again by people who should have protected me. I have been taken advantage of by both men and women. And, like many reading this right now, I believed that it was my fault. I believed that I wasn't enough.

I wasn't enough to be protected
and I wasn't enough to be respected.

My abuse started very young, beginning about the age of four, when I was molested and raped. Then at six years old, continuing on for about the next four years, I experienced being molestation again, but by another female this time. Not only had my innocents been stolen at a young age, but my identity was stolen as well. I became confused as to who I was and where I belonged. The abuse did not happen every day, but it was quite frequent. I knew that it was wrong, but I could not say no. I was scared to disappoint or push her away.

I realize now that my desire to please people was deeply rooted, and stepping outside of this way of life was foreign ground to me. That is how I understood love to be. I did not understand until later on in life why I associated sexual behavior with love, but this was just one way for the enemy to take what was not his.

At the age of fourteen I began messing around with another girl. Again, I knew that it was wrong, but something in me said that this was the only way I would get to experience being wanted by another person. I was so incredibly mistaken.

The abuse and misuse continued on in various forms with several people into my late 20s. I was molested, abused, used, and thrown away like trash.

As I got older, I began abusing myself and I learned manipulation as a technique to get others to love me the way I longed to be loved. I didn't realize that the things I was doing were actually hurting others, but never the less, it was.

I was hurting and I was hungry for love, and I had a skewed idea and understanding what true love was. I became more numb as time crept by and I simply learned how to survive. The saying "hurt people hurt people" is so very true!

Hate Kills

I hated myself. I hated myself for being vulnerable. I hated myself for letting others take advantage of me. I hated myself for being weak. I hated myself for not being good enough. I hated myself. So, I gave myself away.

Every boundary that I may have had about who I was willing to let in or what I was willing to give away was affected by the lack of value I had for myself. "No" was a word that rarely took up residence in my vocabulary, and it was my mission to be tough enough for anything, and the best I could be at everything. That's what was expected of me. The world expected perfection from me, or at least that is how I felt, and so that became the way I found my worth; what I understood worth to be. I became a controlling perfectionist to keep from failing or falling apart. I would push people away before anyone had the chance to hurt me, but still I would end up hurt, and the vicious cycle would start all over again.

Deep down, I did not believe that I was enough. Instead I believed the lie that I was worthless. I did not believe I was worthy of love, so I gave myself away to anyone that would have me.

Over and over again I gave myself away.

I was suffocating, drowning, and had no idea of my identity. I had no idea of who I was. I was invisible, or so I thought. I began to divert all of my pain to hurting myself, and not just with sex.

I began cutting myself and struggled with an eating disorder. I would bang my head against the wall, I would stop eating or drinking all together, sometimes for months at a time among many other things that I did to myself as punishment for not being enough. I would drink myself to sleep and hide myself in drugs, literally trying to end my life. It was my way of punishing myself. It was also my way of pushing Papa God away.

There were times that I would bury myself more in alcohol and drugs. in hopes that He would give up and leave me. I was ashamed. I was embarrassed. I was afraid. I just knew that I had disappointed Him, and although I wanted nothing more than to be held, wanted, and loved by Him, the enemy had me so deeply convinced that I was nothing, and that Papa God wanted nothing to do with me unless it was to punish me.

That was so unbelievably far from the truth!

I did not understand *true* love. I did not understand that I was already loved by my Creator, and that I had *always* been loved by Him. It was difficult for me to understand how He could love me just simply for who I was – His.

I did not understand how He could just overlook or see through all the things I had done and still love me the same. I did not believe that I *could* be loved because of everything that I had done, and everything that had been done to me. I did not believe that I *deserved* to be loved.

Instead, I believed for a long time that I had deserved everything that had happened to me.

My father confirmed this lie one night, whether he intended to or not, when I called him from my front porch in Athens, Georgia to tell him the big news: I was coming out.

I was met with silence, and then the statement I still remember word for word, "I just want to crawl in a corner and cry."

I did not expect him to be on board with my lifestyle, and to be honest, I wasn't even sure myself what I thought. Even though I was in a homosexual relationship and had decided to come out to some of my family, I wasn't so sure deep inside if I was on board. Regardless, the words that followed in that conversation cut deep.

"No wonder all of the things that have happened to you have happened!" He said in a stern voice.

"Ummmmm… what is that supposed to mean, dad?"

"It means exactly what I said, "No wonder the things that have happened to you have happened. God knew this was going to happen. You opened that door a long time ago and cause all this other stuff to happen."

I sat there with tears welling up in my eyes.

"Are you serious??!!" I asked. I was a bit taken back by what I thought I had just heard but I was desperately trying not to jump to conclusions.

"Yes! I'm very serious. I can't believe you."

Still on the phone, I sat up a little more before getting up to pace the road in front of my house. I did not know what to do with myself. I felt not only like a pure disappointment, but also like a failure. And what if he was right? What if.

"Just to clarify that I am not hearing you wrong, taking you wrong, or completely misunderstanding, are you saying that because God knew that this day would come, that I would come out, that He allowed and even caused the abuse, the confusion, the wrecks, the drugs, the suicide attempts, the hurt, the abandonment, the attempted rape, the rape, and everything in between? You are saying that because of this, God was punishing me throughout my entire life for what was to come?" I asked.

"Kayla, I don't think that God would have allowed that stuff any other way. That's exactly what I am saying," was his answer.

"How dare you. I have to go."

As I hung up the phone, my heart had already been ripped to shreds by that single conversation with my dad.

Unfortunately, hell convinced me in that moment, without me even realizing that I had embraced another lie, that he was right, and that my life was my own fault. Because I had chosen to live my life a certain way God had, and was still, punishing me. I was damaged goods. I was worthless, trash, tainted, smaller than, unwanted, weak, screwed up, ugly, imperfect, and unlovable. This was so far from the truth but a very real part of how I saw myself.

It was not my dad's intention to make me feel this way. The truth is that he thought that he was pointing me in the right direction by presenting me with a different perspective. Even though that perspective was judgmental, he believed that what he was saying and doing was right. He knew that what I was doing and who I was portraying myself to be was every bit of wrong and he was scared for my life.

Real talk

I was so far from freedom that I wanted nothing more than to leave this earth, but something in me knew that if I didn't walk in freedom now, there was no way I would walk in freedom after leaving this place. That deep set truth within me in itself shows the grace and the pursuit that Papa has had over me my whole life.

So, what was I to do? I tried several times to end my life, but obviously I failed miserably! (YES!! Thank You Jesus!) I had tried, but He is bigger and the plans He has for my life are far greater than any lie that the enemy can throw at me. Papa God created me as an overcomer!

Years. Years I walked in shame. I lived in an identity battle of not knowing at all who I was, believing who Hell and everyone else said I was, and even who others expected me to be. Confusion about who I was, whether or not I was actually and truly loved, and who I belonged to was a daily battle. It was a battle for my soul and I was too weak to fight it myself, and I was afraid to ask for help or go to Papa. I knew what to do and who to run to but I was afraid of rejection or being abandoned, even by Him. And I simply could not handle being rejected, again. Hell was fighting for me but Papa wasn't giving up!

I was angry and I was hurt. I became bitter. I was angry with myself and with the people that had hurt me. I was angry for not being protected. I was angry for letting myself be angry. And again, the vicious cycle continued.

I became a victim and a survivor of my circumstances rather than an overcomer. That is, until Jesus met me right where I was and assured my heart that He was never going anywhere, that I was worth fighting for, and that freedom was mine if I wanted it.

I couldn't escape Him, but to be honest, I really didn't want to. I wanted to know this Man, Jesus. I wanted to know this love that was chasing me so relentlessly.

Ultimately, this is not about what sexual orientation I did or did not identify with. This is about moving from a place of living a life dictated by others to *stepping into my true identity* because of a God that *refuses* to give up! This is about being loved so radically that giving up that which we think we want becomes our desire, *not an obligation*. This is about being pursued and ravished by a God that doesn't look at your past but *sees your future*. This is about being romanced by a Man that doesn't see you for what you have done but for *who you are*.

This is about a man named *Jesus* who swept me off my feet, taught me about true love, and gave me a new identity wrapped up in Him, not myself or anyone else.

This is about *redemption*!

Radical and outrageous love captured me and shifted everything I thought, felt, and believed about myself. Radical and outrageous love changed my life.

Chapter Six

Insecurity Is Not My Ruler

*I*nsecurity is not a word that 99.9% of us like to admit that we struggle with. Insecurity keeps us bound, often by our past experiences. However it is simply a lack of trust in Papa God and a lack of confidence in yourself in who He created you to be; ultimately it is an uncertainty of who you belong to.

Insecurity believes the lie "I am not good enough." Unfortunately, this feeling is a very real thing that so many people deal with daily. If we take a minute and dissect this, we will notice that insecurity stems from, and is rooted in fear and a lack of intimacy with Jesus!

So how do we fight insecurity? As much as we may not want to hear the truth behind this, the way to fight insecurity is to realize what lies we have been believing about ourselves and letting Holy Spirit rewire our thinking. If we don't address the real problem we will either stay stuck in our insecurities or find ourselves swinging like a pendulum to the other side by being cocky, arrogant, egotistical, and all about yourself.

In order to do this, we start by spending intentional time with Him and letting Him uproot the real issues. It is laying ourselves aside, understanding that when we are focusing on ourselves enough to let insecurity take hold, we are in essence saying that it is all about us and that the power of Holy Spirit to make us confident in who He is and who we are is not enough. Insecurity is not an easy battle and fighting it is not fun. In fact, it can often be uncomfortable, but standing up and fighting is very necessary to overcome insecurity.

I am well acquainted with insecurity. I walked in it for a total of about 28 years. Although Papa God has had much grace over my life and I have experienced so much freedom from insecurity, there are times that I still fight it. I am not immune to being attacked by insecurity just because I have been freed from it. However, speaking truth over these attacks is gold!

When insecurity comes at me, I have learned how to step back, recognize what is happening, and not only pray over it, but command it to go and immediately speak truth and scripture over it: "Thank you Father that I am a daughter of the Most High. I am royalty, created and chosen for such a time as this! I am the head and not the tail. I am above and not beneath. I am beautiful and I am wanted." This is refusing to let the things of the world or the people around me, or the enemy, dictate how I live my life.

If we are to be imitators of Jesus as Paul spoke about in 1 Corinthians 11:2, then we should fight the way He did, yes? How did He fight back? By speaking the Word of His Father. We are to do the same!

Romans 12:2 reminds us to not be conformed to the world, but to be transformed by the renewing of our minds. In order to overcome insecurity, we must allow Him to transform our mind to line up with His and to do this in us, daily!

A friend once taught me a super valuable lesson about this: We can pray something off, out, under or away, all day long, but if we do not fill those places with Holy Spirit, we leave them wide open for attack all over again. We have to get to a place of understanding our authority in Christ and speak truth and life into those places where the enemy either has or tries to occupy.

When we walk in insecurity, how does this affect our life? What happens when we go searching for love when we do not understand what true love is to begin with? As cliché as it is, we end up "looking for love in all the wrong places!" It causes false intimacy and a false sense of identity.

Insecurity says, "I am not good enough. I am a failure. If I could only… If I was better…" among other things. It is not only a lie from Hell, but it creates a victim mentality and you were not created to live as a victim, but as an overcomer!

Insecurity and false intimacy often go hand in hand. False intimacy is a result of insecurity and says "I am not good enough for the real thing and therefore will take whatever I can get." It is a surface level and counterfeit version of true love. When we search for this type of love, we are saying that what Jesus has to offer is not enough.

Laying A Foundation For Insecurity

Next to insecurity and fear, pride is my other least favorite word in the human language and no part of me likes to admit that it sometimes takes up residence in me. Although, it is not in the way you would think. Pride and insecurity actually go hand in hand. They both say, "it is all about me," but when we swim in pity, become fearful of someone not liking us or fearful of failing in general, we are ultimately functioning out of pride. There is a lot of "me" in there!

With as much healing as I have gone through and as much as I HATE to admit it , fear still tries to take hold sometimes, too. I do not live in it, I refuse, but there are things that come up at times that bring me back to this battle. Layers that Papa God wants to get rid of entirely. These things that still try to grip me, or even take control if I were to let them, are the fear of not being wanted, the fear of the closest people in my life walking away, the fear of failing, and the fear of not doing it right.

Ahhhh! Grace, Kayla! Give yourself some grace!

Grace is simply giving compassion and kindness to yourself and others. It is loving yourself. It is loving others, building them up, not tearing them down.

We sometimes have a hard time giving ourselves enough grace to face the things that have happened in our past that bring up these fears, but we must remind ourselves that the past has no hold over your present or the future. The fact is that Jesus has already given us the grace... so take it! Dive in it! Swim in it! Live in it!

We also have to give ourselves grace when facing the things that we have experienced, things that have been done to us, and things that we have done against ourselves or others. We must trust that Jesus is not only going to hold our hand through it, but He also has our front, back, and sides. He has you!!

But you will not go out in haste. Nor will you go as fugitives; for the Lord will go before you, and the God of Israel will be your rear guard.

ISAIAH 52:12

This scripture tells us that He will, without a doubt, not only be there to walk beside us but He goes before us and behind us. It tells us that we have no reason to walk in insecurity, because the God of the universe is literally with us every step of the way. He made you *on* purpose and *for* a purpose, but the enemy wants to convince you that who you were created to be is not enough (not pretty enough, not thin enough, not smart enough, not fast enough, not good enough, etc.) so that you do not live in the fullness of who you were created to be.

Stand up and remind the enemy who he is, who God is, and that you've already won! Do not let him walk on you or convince you that you are less than what you were created for!

I have a beautiful human in my life who I adore beyond words. She is strong, talented in ways that will blow your mind, and loves so deeply and with the heart of Jesus like nobody I know! She has changed my life in ways that I cannot put into words, and her story is beautiful! Her story is not like mine, but it doesn't have to be! Her story is no worse or better than mine, it is just different! She has had her struggles, her battles, and the enemy has tried a billion different ways to ruin her too, but he has failed miserably because she understands who she was created to be and Who she belongs to! Her life changes those around her in the most beautiful ways – it is the life she was created for.

Now, I say all of that to paint a picture of the reality that insecurity can steal the very thing we were made for if we let it. If my person above allowed her insecurities to hold her back, keep her quiet, or shut her down, she would simply just exist. If she compared her story to mine out of insecurity, the world would miss out on what she was created for and what she has been given to release.

The world would miss out on a beautiful piece of history! Insecurity can steal your destiny if you let it. Do not let the enemy steal your destiny because of insecurity. Pick up your sword, the Word, and fight insecurity. Fight your fear.

How do you fight fear? You face it. You take your place in the authority that you were given by Papa God and you remind Hell who you are! It is simple, but not always easy, and yet we were not promised easy, we were simply promised that He would be with us in the midst of the fight.

Looking Fear in the Face

At the age of nineteen, fear began to manifest in some major physical ways. It became so consuming that not only was fear controlling me, but a resulting insecurity from my fear combined with fear itself turned into a battle with shame. Unfortunately, shame can create a foundation for false identity.

When these physical manifestations of fear began to show their face, it was not gradual. In fact, it was so abrupt that I was blindsided by it, and before I knew what had happened, I was completely gripped by fear. It became so bad that I was afraid to walk over a floor vent, put my hand under a faucet, or to even take a shower in fear of something coming out of the faucet. I would not walk by a window if the curtains were open, I would not go near my closet if the light was off at night, I would not go outside after a certain time, and I would not look at myself in the mirror for any extended amount of time because I was afraid of something looking back at me. As a twenty year old, I would even step back several feet from my bed and leap onto it because I was afraid that something would grab me from underneath if I got too close.

I became paralyzed. It was not a fear of man, but I was deathly afraid of the demonic! Hell had gripped me and I was afraid to even fight it. I did not know if I was strong enough, and even though I knew that Papa God was strong enough, it took me time to trust that He would have my back if something "went wrong."

> *And they overcame him because of the blood of the Lamb and because of the word of their testimony, and they did not love their life even when faced with death.*
> REVELATION 12:11

This scripture in Revelation directs us towards how we can overcome fear, and that is by speaking truth and life over ourselves. By standing in and understanding who we are, where our identity lies, and the fact that Hell has no power over true sons and daughters of the Living God, we learn to overcome our fear. As amazing as it sounds, it was not until I actually began walking this out that I was set free from fear.

It's easy to know what to do, but too often we rarely walk out what we know we need to do in order to get the results we want or need. Why? Because the enemy convinces that we can just "think" through the problem, that we can "think" our way into freedom when, in fact, this is not the case at all.

God Himself did not "think" the world into existence. He did not "think" light into existence. He did not "think" mankind into existence. He SPOKE into existence. We hear over and over again that "life and death is in the power of the tongue" (Proverbs 18:21), but how often do we actually believe this, take Him at His word, and use our words the way He intended?

I was sitting on my bedroom floor one night studying the Word with Papa God. I had notes strewed all over the place and my Bible open. I heard Him tell me to flip the page and without thinking or asking questions, I picked my Bible up and flipped the page. I heard Him say stop and read, so I did. What I read literally shifted my entire life in a moment.

The Lord your God is in your midst, a victorious warrior.
He will exalt over you with joy, He will be quiet in His
love, He will rejoice over you with shouts of joy.
ZEPHANIAH 3:17

As I sat there reading this scripture, He began to remind me of Psalm 139:7-11 as well –

Where can I go from Your spirit? Or where can I flee from Your presence? If I ascend to heaven, You are there. If I make my bed in Sheol, behold, You are there. If I take the wings of the dawn, If I dwell in the remotest parts of the sea, even there Your hand will lead me, and Your right hand will lead me. If I say, "surely the darkness will overwhelm me, and the light around me will be night," even the darkness is not dark to You, and the night is bright as day. Darkness and light are alike to you."

There is nowhere that we can go where He is not present, and because this is truth, where He is, darkness cannot stay. Through these scriptures He began to talk to me about walking in authority and remind me that He has my back. Not only does He have my back during the day, but that He sings over me with joy in the night. After that, I immediately began walking in the authority He gave me to stare fear in the face, sometimes quite literally.

I would purposefully walk over vents and even stop to stand on them. I would look at myself in the mirror, hold my hands under the faucet, stand outside at night, and stand by my bed before I got in it. I was not taunting Hell, but standing boldly to remind hell of who I was and Who I belonged to. I would remind the enemy that I was not to be controlled and that when I am weak, my God is strong (2 Corinthians 12:10). It did not take long and the intense fear broke away from my life. But, it did take me acting

out on my faith in Who Papa God says He is, and the fact
that I belong to Him and not the enemy.

Breaking Barriers

With fear no longer a part of my life, doors that I never
imagined possible began to open. It was not long after that
Papa God started to talk to me about going back to school
to get my Bachelor degree. I did not know how this was
going to happen because I never even received my high
school diploma.

I was home schooled for 3 years in high school and
when I went back to public school, I did not have enough
credits to graduate, so instead of sticking it out, I quit.
When the idea of college came up, I had no idea how that
would happen; however, after He confirmed it, I went to
get my GED, scored at a college junior level, applied to two
different private Christian colleges, was accepted to both,
and started school on my 21st birthday. This all happened
within a 3 month period. Again, because of the grace of
Papa God, I was able to look fear in the face and tell it
where to go – back to hell where it belongs.

**Sometimes we just have to look fear in the face
and tell it to go back to hell where it belongs.**

After facing my fears, being accepted to college, and
running into the unknown, my life completely changed. I

was still not sure how God was going to take care of things financially. I had barely received my GED before I dove into college, let alone having scholarship to get me through 4 years of a private Christian college, but Papa God had some crazy plans. He began by asking me to not take out any loans, and to be quite honest, I thought either He or I were crazy.

Over the course of the next four years, Papa God showed up again and again and showed out when it came to my finances. Scholarships and grants would just show up, and there were times that I had no idea how it happened. But He worked it out, and somehow He gave me a measure of faith that even I did not understand, especially because in the rest of my life I was living like Hell.

I came close to being kicked out of college several times due to finances, but I never made it fully out the door. My first semester was both difficult and beautiful, but then the enemy began having His way with my heart once again. As close as I was with Papa God then, I still had so many things from my past that I had not yet dealt with, and it was beginning to show face in a way I had never experienced before.

I became incredibly angry and I had no idea where it was coming from. I began to feel anger and resentment towards God for allowing me to experience the things I had, and I did not know how to handle the feeling and emotions that were so violently emerging from underneath the surface. Those things were supposed to stay buried, or so I thought, but Papa God wanted it all gone.

Instead of running to Him I began falling back into alcohol and drugs again. Very few people knew about what was going on; I did a good job at hiding it. I did a good job at masking the mess that was being made of me on the inside. I would go out every weekend to the bars and the clubs just to escape my reality back on campus and the fact that everything around me there was screaming for me to stop. I got involved in a relationship I had no business being in, and although my heart was gripped with so much conviction I silenced it because I did not believe that I deserved to live a life any better than what I had run into.

My junior year of college took a turn for the worst. I fell into such a deep depression that I stopped eating for nearly 3 months. The thought of food would make me sick to my stomach and anger would rise up in me if I thought about feeding my physical body at all; I felt as though I had to punish myself for amounting to nothing. My friend nearly forced juice down my throat just so that I could live. It came to a point where one of my psychology professors that knew a little bit about what was happening threatened to have me admitted to a hospital if I did not get help.

That scared me enough to try. But, when I arrived at my psych appointment the doctor there told me that there was nothing they could do for me and that I needed to wait 3 more months before they would even attempt to get me help. I left that office feeling even more helpless than I had before I arrived.

On my way back to campus from that meeting, I thought several times of running the car off the side of the road in an attempt to kill myself. Had I not been in my friend's car, leaving her without one, I probably would have tried. Thank God I cared more about leaving her stranded than I did about dying!

I pulled off into a parking lot just moments later because I could barely see through the tears. I sat in that church parking lot for nearly 3 hours screaming, crying, yelling, beating the steering wheel, and pleading for God to do something. I had reached my bottom. There was nowhere to go but up. And He met me there.

No, things were not perfect by any means, and the enemy did not back off completely just because I had made a decision to run towards Papa God, but they got better. I no longer thought of walking across the street and praying that I would get hit by a car to keep from killing myself. I no longer had to lock myself in the closet of my apartment to keep from jumping out my window in hopes that I could end my life quickly from just two stories up.

Death was no longer a constant thought - life was!

Not long after Papa God had once again shifted things, I was presented with a new life as the legal guardian to my fifteen-year-old sister, Abby. My mom was now remarried and because of some issues with their relationship, her living with my mom was simply not an option. My dad, to be frank, could not take care of her. He was not equipped to raise a fifteen-year-old girl on his own, and to be honest, I was not sure that I was either.

I had just turned 23-years-old. I did not have a clue who I was and raising a fifteen-year-old while taking nineteen hours of class, working 4 part time jobs, and relying on my roommate to help out was anything but easy. My friend and I had become parents to our parents, and I became a mother to my little sister. It was not the ideal way to "grow up."

In the midst of all the crazy that happened over the four years of my college experience, I learned a lot about myself and who I did and did not want to be. Although I had made the decision to "come out" to a lot of my family during my senior year of college, I also ran into Papa God in a way that I had never expected.

As I sat in the Mac lab of my college campus one day, He began to talk to me about His plans for me asking if I would join Him. I knew it would not be easy, but I was exhausted from running. The next 2-3 years that followed were some of the hardest that I had ever faced, but it was also the beginning of the end of my running from Him, and learning instead to run into His heart and all that He has had planned for me from the start. He taught me how to thrive, not just survive. He taught me how to live as an overcomer.

We do not live as victims but as victors. Letting Papa burn out the things that control our lives is nothing but beautiful! He crushes everything that isn't of Him!! Love and intimacy destroys fear and insecurity!

So, why do we too often stay bound in insecurity, false intimacy, fear, pride, or any other spirit that keeps us from walking in our true identity?

Brace yourself!! Are you ready for this one??

We do not trust the very One that has our lives in His hand. We do not trust His opinion, His thoughts, or His love for us over others. We do not trust that He will walk through healing with us. We do not trust that He has our heart in the palm of His hand. We do not trust that He will never hurt us.

Laughing Is The Best Part

I was accepted to go on the World Race (an 11-month missions trip to 11 different countries) in January 2016. However, during training camp, Papa God called me away in a different direction. I was utterly confused by the last minute change because He had already asked so much of me. I had already resigned from my very good paying job, given all of my things away, and sold my car. It did not make sense but I had given Him my "yes" no matter what, so when He asked, I walked away from the Race.

After leaving, I wasn't sure what I was going to do. So much had changed so quickly. Although I knew fully who I was and Who I belong to, I began to question myself. I questioned how others would view me. I wondered if I was enough. Insecurity began to creep in again but because He taught me who I am in Him, and that I do not have to accept insecurity from the enemy, I fought it and overcame it!

Papa God used that season to teach me what it means to hold onto joy no matter what, to laugh even when everything looks like it is falling apart, to worship when you don't know what to do next, to praise Him even when every voice is coming at you telling you everything but the truth, and to be still and know that He is God even when nothing makes sense. It was a season of learning how to maintain joy in the midst of crazy. He continues, and will continue, to bring me into a new understanding of who He is, who I am in Him, and who we are together.

There is a song that Jesus Culture does called "Pursuit." Some of the lyrics say, "Strip everything away till all I have is You. Undo the veils till all I see is You." When we say or sing these kinds of words, He takes us seriously. He took me seriously when I did!

The first thing He seems to tackle and work at stripping away is fear at the core because His desire for us is to know Him and know who we are above anything and everything else. It can be uncomfortable, but when we walk in who He created us to be – simply His – we will no longer be walking in fear, and the insecurities will fall away. However, we have to be willing to let go of the places we have been comfortable sitting.

When Papa God shut the doors to the World Race, I got angry. I got angry at Him because He changed it up on me, again. And I got angry at myself because I thought I knew what I was supposed to do and somehow got it wrong. That's what I believed. I let the enemy use me as his playground until a friend reminded me that this was just a thing and that this is nothing to Papa. In fact, chances are, He has something else planned.

SHOCKER!
Gasps for breath

Once I took a deep breath and calmed down, it was much easier to see.

"Spend time investing in family," He said.

"But God! This doesn't make sense! I don't have a job! I don't have much of anything any more. What the heck am I supposed to do??"

"Trust Me," He says.

"Of course! Why didn't I think of that before?!?!" I said in a very sarcastic tone.

After throwing my temper tantrum (let's face it, I wasn't getting my way so acting like a 5 year old seemed appropriate at the time) I suddenly realized what He was about to do. But, was I on board??

At first, no, not at all! I was angry about it because I wanted what I wanted and I wasn't getting it. But after some long and extensive conversations with Him, I began to understand, and everything inside me became really excited for what I knew He was about to do in my life, and my family's life.

See here is the thing - when we can overcome fear and insecurity and refuse to let pride take hold of our lives in any way, Papa God can work and do what only He can do in a deeper way with no obstruction or reservation. But, we cannot overcome those things on our own.

We HAVE to totally and completely rely on Him no matter what. We have to make a decision to hand it over to Him, regardless of what it cost us.

REALITY:

That cost is everything and ALL of us, our yes at 100%. When we give Him our yes, He takes us at our word. Step into your identity as a son and daughter and walk in all He has for you. Walk in wholeness. It has been given; it is done! We don't have to do anything to win His love or approval. We already have it. Is that enough for you? Are you willing to fight insecurity, give Him your yes, mean it, allow Him to strip everything away so He can do what only He can in your life?

Instead of your shame you will have a double portion, and instead of humiliation they will shout for joy over their portion. Therefore they will possess a double portion in their land, everlasting joy will be theirs.
Isaiah 61:7

Chapter Seven

Shame On Shame

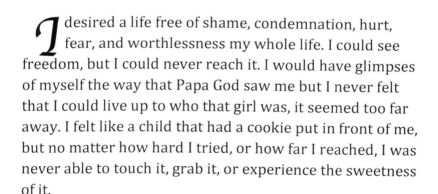

I desired a life free of shame, condemnation, hurt, fear, and worthlessness my whole life. I could see freedom, but I could never reach it. I would have glimpses of myself the way that Papa God saw me but I never felt that I could live up to who that girl was, it seemed too far away. I felt like a child that had a cookie put in front of me, but no matter how hard I tried, or how far I reached, I was never able to touch it, grab it, or experience the sweetness of it.

This was nothing but a lie from the enemy, of course. The truth was that I could have the cookie;. I could live in that freedom as a part of the prize that I receive because of the life and love of Jesus in me! But first I had to get lose from the rope that had me tied to the boat that I had been traveling in for so long.

When we are carrying or pulling weight that does not belong to us, it keeps us from reaching the places we were created to go. I was, for the longest time, tied up to shame and could not seem to get loose from it. It seemed that every time I would get close to getting rid of it and letting go, it would come at me with a vengeance. As a result I stayed quiet, kept my mouth shut, and believed the lie that I had nothing to give and nothing to offer. Hell tried to steal my destiny, and for far too long succeeded in stealing my voice.

The Face of Shame

Let's look at what shame actually is.

According to Psychology Today's Dr. Joseph Burgo, shame is "a painful feeling arising from the consciousness of something dishonorable, improper, ridiculous, etc., done by oneself or another."

This is exactly what so many of us have or do struggle with on a daily basis. Whether it be from something you have done or something that has been done to you, chances are that every person reading this right now has faced shame in some form and at some point in your life.

Perhaps you have done drugs and you are terrified of who you became while doing that line, smoking that joint, taking that pill, or trying out the latest fad for the newest high while still unwilling to admit that the person you have become is not who you dreamed of growing up to be. So, you hold your head down and begin to walk in shame's footsteps.

You lost your virginity to that guy you barely knew at sixteen because you thought that he just might like you just enough to stick around if you give him what he wants. But then you realize that was all lust and fantasy and you have given part of you away. The enemy convinces you that you are now damaged goods and unworthy of true love, so you begin to walk in shame's shadow.

You were molested and or raped as a child by someone you cared about, and who you thought cared about you. Whether that person was a friend of the family, a father, stepfather, grandfather, brother, or an uncle, you were taken advantage of, but somehow the enemy has convinced you that it was your fault. That if you had just been better, it wouldn't have happened. If you would have just not been born part of that family, then maybe you would have slid by the abuse. If you were worthy enough of love or worth protecting that just maybe it would not have happened. And the enemy convinces you with one syllable at a time that you are nothing and that there is no way you could ever tell anyone because you would either ruin their lives or ruin your own. You fear that if anyone were to find out they will blame you, so you hold your head down and you walk in shame's footsteps.

You began drinking because it was your one and only escape from the reality of your past. One small drink turned into a few, and a few into many, that many turned into bottles, and still it seems as if your past is catching up to you and you cannot run fast enough to make it to safety, so you down one more. The enemy convinces you that you are nothing but a failure, a worthless piece of flesh that deserves nothing more than the things that have been done to you. He convinces you that you are a failure of a mother, a father, a friend, or even a failure as a child of God. And so you hold your head down and take one more drink in hopes that all the thoughts that run rampant through your mind will one day take a backseat and quite for just enough time to believe that you are not crazy. You walk in shame's shadow because you don't deserve any more than what you have lived.

As real as shame is, it is nothing but a straight up brutal attack from the enemy himself. 1 Peter 5:8 tells us that our adversary, or Satan, prowls around *like a roaring lion*, seeking out someone to devour. The enemy likes to try and hurt us and take us for all that we have simply because he knows our destinies. He knows Who we ultimately belong to and shame is just one way he will attempt to destroy us because he understands the power of shame.

However, the power of God is no match for shame! Because here is the truth...you may have done those drugs, but you can still be that man or woman you dreamed of being as a child. You may have lost your virginity at 16, but that does not in the slightest bit means you are damaged goods! You are, my dear, beautiful in every way and worthy of true love! You may have been molested or raped, but it was not your fault! You are worthy, SO WORTHY, of love and protection!!! You may not understand it now, but you were kept by your heavenly Father and are sitting here reading this right now.

Feel your heartbeat?
That is purpose.

You are beautiful!
Shame has no place in your life!

You may have turned to alcohol, bottle after bottle in an attempt to run, but you cannot outrun the One that loves you enough to give His life for you. He wants to see you walk in complete freedom from your past hurts and confusion, and He desires to pursue your heart so fiercely.

You do not belong in fear's shadow! You belong in the shadow of wings of the Almighty! That is protection. That is safety. That is escape. When we run from our past, the things that have been done to us or the things we have done, we are letting those things have control of our destiny, our children's destiny, and our family's destiny.

Kept Silent

One way in particular that the enemy tried destroying me was with my story of homosexuality. It took me a good bit of time before I would share with anyone my past because it seemed that every time I did, people would turn their back on me, compare me now to the girl I once was, or immediately expect me to be that girl I had been before. This cultivated a lot of shame, not only in the things that I did myself, but also from a history of things that had been done to me. I felt like a failure.

Shame does just that – it calls out faults and failures.

Much like insecurity, shame tells you that you are not good enough, pretty enough, talented enough, fast enough, smart enough... that who you are is not enough. Shame says that you are the mistake and that you don't ultimately matter.

Being focused on one's self is the product of shame. And it is exactly where the enemy likes to keep you. If he can keep you focused on yourself, then your focus is not on the One who made you to walk in freedom from shame; It will keep you quiet and from walking in your true identity. Any time that you are kept quite, shut up, or shut down, the enemy is robbing the world of you and what you were created to release. It is also a way to keep you bound and held back from stepping fully into your destiny.

Telling my dad about being gay is a perfect example of how feeling shame, failure, and worthlessness was burnt into me. I felt like a disappointment, shut down, and continued to bury myself in self-hatred and walk in shame in even greater ways.

One thing I have learned over the years is that Hell is very intentional in how it attacks. Hell knows and understand who you are and will use your vulnerabilities to wear you down. Hell is given the name enemy on purpose! But because Hell is intentional in its attacks, we must also be intentional in guarding our hearts, minds, bodies, and souls. Sometimes this can mean giving up the very thing that we find our comfort in, if it is anything but Jesus. It also means giving up our fears, failures, and shame and trusting Papa God to take care of our hearts.

Yes, this can be much easier said than done, but it starts with surrender. Shame can cause a snowball effect in your life if you allow it; however, there are ways to overcome the shame and release the hold that it allows the enemy to have on your heart.

One of the best ways to fight shame is to get real, raw, and vulnerable. Because Hell will try to use your vulnerabilities against you – the things you think or feel - it is important to stare that fear in the face and get vulnerable with those you trust.

Vulnerability is not necessarily easy. In fact, even for benefit's sake very few people actually allow themselves to be open and exposed to the possibility of getting hurt, let alone for the sake of healing.

We can look at Jesus' life and the vulnerability He exuded as an example. He was vulnerable in the deepest of ways and He still is vulnerable with us today. He allowed people of His time to see Him for everything that He was... in all His humanity.

One instance in which we see His vulnerabilities exposed is in Matthew 26:39 when Jesus was in the Garden of Gethsemane the night of His capture. He was on His knees before the Father asking if this cup could pass from Him, to please let it be done another way. Jesus knew that He was about to go to the cross. He knew that what He was about to face would be excruciating in every way. Although He knew the death He was about to face, He asked Papa God for it to pass Him if it could. But, Jesus humbled Himself to dwell among humanity and to bridge the gap for relationship and restoration of man back to the Father. Because of this, He followed His prayer with, "yet not My will but Yours be done." Jesus was in such distress that He was literally sweating drops of blood. This is such a beautiful picture of vulnerability in which He shows us that it is okay to bare our souls, and to expose the things we are feeling with those that have been put in our lives!

Vulnerability is not weakness! I heard a speaker at a conference not too long ago ask how many people in the audience think of vulnerability as weakness when they

think of doing something "vulnerable." Out of 500
attendees, about ¾ of the room raised their hands. The
speaker then followed up with "How many in here, when
you see vulnerability, think that it is pure courage?" The
entire room raised their hands. There is a disconnect with
how we perceive vulnerability when demonstrated by
others compared to ourselves, and we need to change
that!

You were created a warrior, to courageously stand and
fight, to wield your authority that has been given to you,
trusting that Papa God will protect your heart as you heal.
This is not to suggest you should just run to anyone who
will listen; in fact, the Word talks about this very thing.

Solomon tells us in Proverbs 4:23 to guard our heart
and later 1 Corinthians 15:33 tells us "Do not be deceived:
"Bad company ruins good morals." We see also in
Proverbs 12:15 that "the way of a fool is right in his own
eyes, but a wise man is he who listens to counsel."

We must seek *Godly* council in order to grow and
mature into the person we were created to be, not just the
council of anyone. Ask Papa God to bring that person into
your life that will speak truth, life, encouragement, love,
restoration, peace, and wholeness if you do not already
have them, and stay away from the ones that pass
judgment, their own views and ideas, or unbiblical
principle. Those things just cause discord and confusion
and are purely dangerous.

Freedom Is Possible

As time went on and I made new friends, I would avoid telling them of my past at all costs because it seemed that any time I would tell someone, they would distance themselves. It was difficult for me to trust anyone with my heart. I hated vulnerability.

It became increasingly difficult over time, nearly impossible rather, for me to share my story. I became fearful of people walking out of my life, constantly. I feared being abandoned by someone else in my life. This made it very challenging to make friends or let anyone into the vicinity of my heart. It was not until I really stepped into vulnerability and let Papa God take over that I experienced true freedom from the shame of my past.

There *is* freedom from your past! The question is how bad do you want to walk in that freedom and what are you willing to lay down – pride, selfishness, fear, control, etc. – in order to walk in the freedom you have available to you? How hard are you willing to fight for your life? You do not have to live in the shadow of the things that have been done to you or the things that you have done yourself. There is freedom in embracing the hardship of healing, pushing through, and refusing to let the enemy win. There is freedom in walking out the pain of healing and trusting that Papa God will do what He promised in your life!

When Papa God began digging deeper and taking me through the process of healing and forgiveness, not only with the people that hurt me but also for myself, I had to make an intentional decision to push through regardless of how hard it was. I had to make a decision to stand in who I was created to be, put the enemy on lockdown, and refuse to take hold of the lies that were being thrown at me.

It can be incredibly easy to jump onboard with the lies that the enemy speaks to us in our dreams, as we are waking up, or as we are going through our day. Sometimes it is much easier to just agree with him rather than use energy to fight for the freedom that Papa God has given. However, if we take hold of the lies that tell us, "You're not good enough," "It's all your fault," "You're worthless," etc., even for just a moment, then we are giving the enemy a foothold and an opportunity to have his way in our lives.

I refuse to let the enemy have possession of my life; I refuse to give hell the satisfaction of winning any part of the war over my life. I refuse to lie down and surrender to anyone but my God.

Papa God placed a few beautiful people in my life that gave me the love and encouragement I needed in order to fight shame, push through, begin to share my story, and walk out healing in an even greater way than I believed I ever could. It was not easy, in fact it was scary as Hell at first, but with it came so much freedom and joy! I now have some amazing humans that I share my life with on a daily basis, even from 8,000 miles away that make it easy for me to be vulnerable. I have healed in crazy ways because of Papa God through them, and now I stand and look fear and shame in the face because it no longer has a hold on my life!

Instead of your shame there shall be a double portion; instead of dishonor they shall rejoice in their lot; therefore in their land they shall possess a double portion; they shall have everlasting joy.

ISAIAH 61:7

My dear, the things you have done or the things that have been done to you does not determine your identity or your destiny. Only the One above does that, and He died for you years ago so that you could walk in freedom and wholeness.

Do not let the fear of man hold you in shame.
Do not let the enemy keep you from your destiny.
Do not let Hell steal your joy or your life.

You were created for so much more than to walk in shame's shadow!
So dive into vulnerability,
trusting that Papa God has your back!!

Chapter Eight

Face to Face with Love

*I*t is a beautiful thing, being pursued.

For the first 28 years of my life, pursuit meant something very different to me than it does now. Pursuit was not something pure that I looked forward to; in fact, pursuit made me exceptionally uncomfortable. In my experience up until that point, pursuit always took advantage of my heart. Pursuit meant perversion and a counterfeit version of true love. Because I had experienced so much pain when it came to this, I avoided it with almost anyone, even Papa God. I did not realize the beauty that lies in God's true and pure pursuit of me and my heart.

It amazes me more every day of the relentless love that He has for His sons and daughters! After all the running and hiding that I did, He still continued to chase me down until I surrendered. This was not because He was trying to force me to surrender, but because He loves so relentlessly that He stopped at nothing to have my heart. The beautiful piece of this is that once I surrendered, He never stopped pursuing. In fact, He continued (and continues) as if He had never caught me.

You are no exception, my friend! The fact that you are reading this right now shows His beautiful pursuit of your heart. He wants you to know that He WANTS you! He desires you!

Love Unconditional

I was afraid of intimacy in any way with anyone, particularly men because I had been wounded so deeply by so many of them. I tried my best not to bundle them all in the same group, but it was difficult for me to differentiate the good ones from the bad, except for a few that had proven pure in my life.

I want to tell a story first about a man that captivated my heart from the time I was born and never once took advantage of me. Instead, he loved me unconditionally. This man acted as a father, a brother, and a friend. This man is my uncle Tim.

My uncle Tim is, by far, one of the most amazing men I know. No, he is not perfect in the least bit, but he loves with the heart of Papa God in the deepest ways! He portrays love, strength, selflessness, and he is one of the funniest guys I know.

Tim does not know the full impact he has had on my
life. In fact, I am not sure that he knows the impact he has
had on so many people beyond myself. His unwavering
and unconditional love for me kept me together when all I
wanted to do was disappear and die. Papa God would not
only remind me of His love for me, but He would give me
flashbacks of Tim loving on me growing up, not with any
agenda or expectation of how I should be, but just pure,
true love.

My aunt Angela is no exception. She has held me up
and supported me when I was ready to give up,
encouraged me when I felt like a failure, pushed me when
I wanted to quit, picked me up when I was crumbling, and
has loved me with the most unconditional love I have ever
experienced. Angela has never one time questioned the
things that Papa God has, or is, doing in my life, but she
cheers me on and reminds me that I was created for right
now, for this particular time in history.

Some of my favorite family memories are going to see
them during college breaks, sitting on the couch with Tim
watching the game (whatever game was on), or hanging
out with Angela in the kitchen just talking about life. They
never one time treated me any different than their own
kids, except that I didn't get in trouble :).

They have never asked anything from me, and they
have had high, but never unrealistic, expectations. Instead,

they have dreamed with me and encouraged because they know I am capable.

Is this not the type of relationship that anyone with a breath in their lungs longs to have?

> To be loved unconditionally and
> without crushing expectation?

My Aunt and Uncle provided this example to me in the earthly form, but Papa God only cares for us more so! You are relentlessly pursued by a loving God, but if you are unwilling to surrender to Him, or if you are not willing to lay down your pride, expectations, or your past, you will not gain all the benefits of being caught by love.

Surrender

Surrender is not an easy thing to do. In fact, it can be incredibly painful, mostly because it hurts our pride. As humans we like to be in control, and when we surrender and wave that "white flag" we are admitting that we can no longer do this thing called life on our own. We can no longer live our own way, but would rather lay it down for something better. This can often sting, but it is a necessary part of the journey in order to live and walk fully in who you were created to be. We must first die to ourselves.

When we surrender to Papa God, we are giving over

our rights to our lives - to control our future, our destiny, and ourselves - and instead we are letting Him lead our every step. We are agreeing to give Him complete control.

To surrender is to relinquish all control of every aspect of our lives, and submit to His authority in every part of our lives.

For whoever wishes to save his life will lose it, but whoever loses his life for My sake and the gospel's will save it.

MARK 8:35

When we try to hold onto control of our lives, of our destiny, we are in essence saying that we know better, and that the God of the universe does not deserve the rights over what He created. However, when we choose to surrender everything, we actually gain everything! If we could shift our perspective to see the goodness that is wrapped up in full surrender to His perspective, it would be the easiest thing to do.

But because we can't see this so easily all the time, it takes a lot of trust and courage to surrender.

There are stories written all throughout the Bible about surrender and the benefits of surrendering. Jesus is a perfect example. We see in the Garden of Gethsemane that Jesus surrenders His very life to Papa God, and we can use that as an understanding of how we also should have the same surrender. Philippians 2:5-8 says:

Have this attitude in yourselves, which was also in Christ Jesus, who, although He existed in the form of God, did not regard equality with God a thing to be grasped, but emptied Himself, taking the form of a bondservant, and being made in the likeness of men. Being found in appearance as a man, He humbled Himself by becoming obedient to the point of death, even death on a cross.

Surrender calls for sacrifice. Christ sacrificed His life for each of us because of His love. He did not compromise Himself or His authority, but He did sacrifice His position to take on the form of man so that we could know Him in deeper ways.

As time has gone on and we have made it to the 21st century, our generation has taken the idea of sacrifice and often confuses it with compromise. You were not created to compromise your values and morals, or your understanding of who you are, who you belong to, or what you were created for! The world will ask that of you, but Papa God asks for a different kind of surrender; He asks for a whole sacrifice of your life to Him so that He can mold you into the person He created you to be for His glory.

A beautiful friend, Bailey Rushlow, puts it like this:

"There is a huge difference between compromise and sacrifice. Compromise is laying down the value of who you are called to be in Christ and setting yourself up for failure by fitting into the "one size fits all" mold that the world tries to put you in. It is laying down your character and who you were called to be, as opposed to sacrifice, which is not lying down or devaluing your expectation but raising them while laying down your pride at the same time. The world tries to tell you they go hand in hand when in fact they are complete opposites. Christ sacrificed; the world compromises."

We are told in Romans 12 not to be conformed to the world, but rather transformed by the renewing of our mind. This is because He wants His very best for you. When you compromise, you are living for less than you were created for.

Everything Changed

When I began counseling, I was fearful of losing myself. I was afraid of surrender. Counseling meant that I would have to be vulnerable and that I would be exposed, naked. It meant that I would be stripped bare for the world to see and that scared the hell out of me.

Surrender took on a whole new meaning when I stepped in that office for the first time, but coming face to face with love was waiting for me there.

Surrender requires trust and faith in the one you are surrendering to. It is trusting that your life in the palm of another's hands is not going to be taken advantage of or hurt. Once I grabbed ahold of the truth that this is what Papa God wanted from me, my heart began to soften, and surrender was something I was happy to give. Sure it is hard at times, but that is when I had to learn that He will guard my heart and protect me.

I went every week for nearly sixteen months to see Alissa and confront and attack the hold that the enemy had on my life. It was the best decision I ever made – to surrender to Papa God and trust that He knew what He was doing. Within those sixteen months, I went through healing that I never imagined possible. I learned about myself, who I truly was, and what I was created for. I realized that the freedom I knew was nothing compared to the freedom I was created for.

As time went on and old memories emerged and unfolded, I understood a little more of the depth of Papa God's love for me and how He kept me my whole life. I recognized how strong He created me to be. I realized how beautiful He made me. I began to believe that I am enough; I am enough for what He created me for. But none of this came from just sitting in the corner of my room hiding away from the rest of the world and repeating over and over again "I think I can, I think I can," or "I'm good enough, I'm good enough." It was not because I faked it till I made it, although I tried that. It did not come by talking myself into believing it.

It came by surrender to my Jesus. It came by surrendering my heart and saying that I was going to fight and push through no matter what. It came by my relentless pursuit of Jesus and refusing to live for less than what I was made for.

In February 2015 I attended a 4-day event called the Encounter Training in Nashville, TN. The purpose of this event was to discover who God had created me to be beyond the wounds of my past. During those four days, more happened than I can verbalize. I was completely set free. I attended the event trusting that Papa God was going to do something great, crazy even, but I received that weekend I never imaged possible!

As the weekend progressed, 2,000 pounds of memories and wounds came to the surface. The anger and bitterness that I had been holding onto vanished that last night, and I understood for the first time how I had been held back and stuck for so long. It was because I never fully surrendered all that I was and all that I had been carrying and holding onto for all those years.

The enemy had me so paralyzed in bondage that I could not see how trapped I was, and when I did see it, I was too afraid to admit that I was being held prisoner. I was afraid to admit that I did not know how to fix it myself. I experienced a freedom that weekend that I had never known before, but I was going to soon face opposition in many ways.

Hold Fast

People are afraid of what they do not understand.

I was now walking in crazy freedom and a newfound joy but because I had lived so angry and bitter for so long, the people around me expected this "transformation" not to last more than several days at best. However, when those days turned into weeks and then into months, those people began to criticize and mock me. Things such as "Kayla, I think I liked you better when you were pissed off all the time!" or "Why in hell is she so happy all the time?" were being said, along with friends doubting or expressing their concern of my change because they did not know me anymore.

It was during these times especially that I had to hold fast and trust that Papa God knew what He was doing and that I was not missing Him completely. I was now happy and joyful, and people were dropping out of my life?

I did not want to give up the people in my life that I loved! It hurt my heart to watch them walk away because they did not understand what was happening in my life. But, I could not stop pursuing Jesus because of fear of man, fear of abandonment, or fear of being alone anymore. I had done that one too many times and had now experienced Him in ways I never had before that didn't allow me to turn back. I refused to let go of Him and His love, even if it meant I lost everyone else in the process.

I did not owe anyone an explanation. The only one I owed anything to was Papa God! He gave His life for me... my surrender to Him seemed so small in comparison. He asked for my heart, my surrender, and my life and it was all that I had, so, I gave Him my "yes" willingly.

The moment that I threw my hands up and surrendered all that I did have, my life took a radical shift and it happened quickly. It was in the midst of pursuing who He is, that I ran into my own freedom. I found the strength and courage to fight for my relationship with Him. I found the strength and courage to stand up for what I believed, and in who I was created to be.

I know that surrender is not easy and you may be reading this wondering how you can even begin to let go, because so much has held you back and weighed you down for so long. It may seem impossible. But, I promise you that it is not impossible! In fact, that is exactly what the enemy wants you to believe – that it is impossible. But, you were created a warrior! You were created to take hell by storm and change the world for the kingdom. You were created for this time, right now. You were created an overcomer. You were created for kingdom!

I only thought I knew what freedom was before really experiencing what it can be. The saying "you don't know until you know" seems silly, but it is true! I did not know true freedom until I KNEW true freedom, until I experienced it for myself. I ran from Papa God and my destiny for so long but He never quit pursuing me! He pursued my heart relentlessly and as soon as I surrendered, turned, and began running towards Him, I not only encountered freedom but I came face to face with Love Himself.

He has the most beautiful face.

Chapter Nine

Freedom in Forgiveness

"*A*fter everything that you have been through – all the hurt, the abuse, the pain, the let downs, and the abandonment – after all that, how in hell can you forgive?"

I have been asked this question a number of times. I have asked myself this question as well. My answer is one that I've wrestled with, but that wrestling solidified and is now what anchors me: Jesus. He took me through the healing I needed at the exact moment I needed it. He saved my life!

Forgiveness is not a walk in the park, and it definitely is not purple daisies or warm sunshine. Forgiveness is a choice that you make every day. It is something that you set your mind to and chose to do not necessarily because it's "the right thing to do," but because it is necessary for a life of purpose and freedom.

Forgiveness is also not something that is done easily, especially if you have long and deep rooted hurt, but it is still possible. I can tell you from experience. It was a long and painful road for me up to the time that I stopped and let go, but once that happened, everything changed!

Dying to self – it still hurts.

Oh, but the Process!

For the longest time, 29 years to be exact, I was convinced that I understood what forgiveness was. I thought that I understood its importance and the impact that true forgiveness cultivates. But I didn't. I did not understand how freedom would literally take over my life once I truly forgave those that hurt, abandoned, and abused me.

The process of forgiving was not an easy one. In fact, there are still times that I have to step back and remind myself that I gave up control and that it is not my job to hold unforgiveness, but to love no matter what. To be honest, I hated the idea of forgiving. I hated the thought of having to give up the "right" to hold the people responsible, even if just in my mind, for the things they did to me. I hated the idea of giving up my right to hurt.

My biggest issue with forgiveness, however, was trusting that God was who He says He is and trusting that He would have my back, stick up for me, heal my heart, and avenge me even. It was hard trusting but I was out of options. I did not want to live life the same anymore. I had to have freedom.

When we hold onto unforgiveness, we are in essence giving that person or persons control over our lives. We are making space for them to dictate our emotions, our fears, our relationships, and ultimately giving them rule over our identity.

There's a passage in the Bible that even likens having hate in your heart to murder:

Everyone who hates his brother is a murderer; and you know that no murderer has eternal life abiding in him.
1 John 3:15

I did not understand the true reality of this until I actually relinquished my control and got free from this thing that was killing me. Just to add a little more understanding to the magnitude of this short verse is how it correlates with one of the Ten Commandments in Exodus 20:13 when it says – *"You shall not murder."* Unforgiveness is walking in the sin of murder. No, it may not be in the same way that we understand murder to be, but it is nonetheless murder.

If you will, take a visual trip with me for just a minute. (I apologize for the morbid explanation, but I feel it necessary and I want to give a sense of the gravity of unforgiveness.)

Imagine the person that hurt or abused you - verbally, emotionally, mentally, physically, or even spiritually - sitting in front of you. Imagine them hunched over dead. Now imagine the unforgiveness in your heart and how much you want them to suffer for what they did to you, for the hurt, the anger, and the bitterness welling up inside of you. Now imagine picking that person up and strapping their dead body to yours. This is what happens when we hold onto unforgiveness. We are attaching that person to ourselves, giving them power.

Now imagine with me a bit further. When you have unforgiveness, do you not feel the weight of that "hurt" on your back? It is because you refuse to let them go and that weight becomes heavier, weighing you down, exhausting you – taking energy from your life because you are allowing it to live with you.

The longer you hold onto that person, onto that unforgiveness, that dead body becomes fused to your own, entangled with your thoughts and beliefs. You have now allowed that hurt, anger, and bitterness to take root. Your life begins to smell of these things because you grow what you feed. If you are feeding these things because you refuse to let go of control, they overflow and before you know it, your life is rotting.

I tell you this to give you an understanding of the danger of holding onto unforgiveness.

Forgiving is not necessarily for the other person, although this can sometimes happen, but forgiveness is for yourself, your eternal life, and your relationship with Papa God. Matthew 6:14-15 is very clear as to the reward of forgiveness and the consequence of unforgiveness.

For if you forgive others for their transgressions, your heavenly Father will also forgive you. But if you do not forgive others, then your Father will not forgive your transgressions.

These are words that were spoken by Jesus on the Sermon on the Mount, so I would imagine that it is grossly important and something that we should take very seriously.

Finally I Surrender

One thing I have learned is that forgiving someone does not mean that it is wrong for me to still feel angry or hurt for what has happened. It does not mean that I am at fault or that I condone the actions of the person that hurt me. For the longest time I thought that if I forgave certain people it was excusing them for the things they did. And in a way, that is what forgiveness is – taking them off death row, pardoning them - but it does not make what they did any less real or wrong, or your hurt any less valid.

Forgiving is not a free pass for someone to take up

residence in your life. I had to learn that forgiving did not mean that I had to cultivate a relationship with the person that hurt me. I do not have to sit and have coffee or a nice chat with the man that molested me, or the guy that violently raped me. It does not mean that I agree with or condone the actions of that person. It does not even mean that what happened is now null and void like it never happened. Forgiveness simply means that you choose to be free.

When you forgive, the person that had so much control over your emotions and your life loses that control, and you begin to walk in the freedom Papa God gives. When we let go, we give Papa God control to do what He will to avenge us in HIS timing.

Revenge is not my job. Love is my job.

Then Peter came and said to Him, "Lord, how often shall my brother sin against me and I forgive him? Up to seven times?" Jesus said to him, "I do not say to you, up to seven times, but up to seventy times seven."
MATTHEW 18:21-22

In this passage there are several factors that play into why Jesus said seventy times seven but one is that Peter was asking Jesus what the perfect number would be to forgive because, after all, seven is a significant number to Papa God. It actually symbolizes perfection. However, in

this passage, Jesus is telling the crowd that we should not
hold a tally against our brother that has sinned against us.
Again, we go back to Matthew 5:48 –

*Therefore you are to be perfect, as your heavenly Father
is perfect.*

We are to walk out love, and not just towards those we
love and adore who make it easy to love them, but also
towards those who are difficult to love; We have to love
those who may be unwilling to sacrifice themselves or
their ways or those that continue to try and hurt us over
and over again. If we are functioning out of Father's heart,
the attacks may not be any fewer or less relevant, but we
do see those things from a different perspective, from
Papa God's perspective. This brings about even more
healing within us.

Just a bite

It took a couple years to let go of the layers of pain that
consumed my life, but I finally got to a place in my journey
of healing that I was able to drop off a tear-soaked paper
of thoughts to a man who had been one of the biggest
contributors to the pain of my past.

Papa God had been asking me for a while to sit and
write a letter to my Pawpaw. He understood that writing
was my way of processing. However, I did not want to. I

did not want to give Pawpaw the satisfaction of knowing that I forgave him. Childish? Maybe, but that was real. One morning changed everything, though.

I walked out of my bedroom and into my kitchen for some breakfast that morning. As I passed by my dinning room table, I felt a sudden shift and an innate desire to sit and write this letter that I had been avoiding for some time. Instead of making it to the kitchen, I sat down at my computer and began writing.

The next 3 hours were full of tears, yelling, hurt, pain, and then it happened...I began to feel Papa God's heart for him. No, it does not excuse the things he did to me, our family, and countless others, but it did help me to see him completely different, not as my enemy, but rather as a son that had surrendered to the wrong things, the wrong people, and the enemy. I now felt sadness for him. It was not a place I had ever been before.

As I continued typing, Papa God helped me to articulate what I had been wanting to say to him– what I am sure so many others had wanted to say for the past 15 years. I was not disrespectful, but I was very real, raw, vulnerable, and truthful. To be quite honest, I had no intention of giving him this letter when I wrote it. However, I did put it in an envelope, address it, seal it up, and put it in my purse. I held onto that letter for 2 weeks and then as I passed my mailbox one day, I dropped it in the outgoing box. That was it. There was no turning back. All I could do was pray that my heart was heard and that maybe one day, that relationship would be restored.

One of the beautiful things about forgiveness is that we do not have to come face to face with those that we forgive. It is not always necessary, nor is it always safe. So, if you feel like you need to do so, I would encourage you to take someone with you that you trust.

Sending that letter was not easy, but I felt it was necessary. I wanted him to understand why I had kept my distance for so many years and I wanted him to know that despite all the wrong, all the hurt, and all the pain, I forgave him. I also wanted him to know that I love him. Despite everything, he is still my Pawpaw. He was put in my life for a reason and nothing would ever change that.

God had started to do a crazy work in my heart, and I felt the need to share that with him. No, it did not completely repair our relationship, but that was okay because the day I wrote that letter was the day that things began to shift in my heart.

The day I sent that letter off was the day that my heart felt freer than it had in a long time. The freedom that I felt after this happened with my Pawpaw though, was nothing compared to what was coming!

You Can't Love Without Forgiveness

If we want to walk in who we were truly created to be, we have to first understand this simple but deep truth: we were created by love, for love, to release love as though

Jesus were functioning through us at all times. It is impossible to love without forgiveness, though. Let's look at a couple different examples of love trumping hate, hurt, bitterness, and anger, and ultimately unforgiveness.

Jesus is our first and foremost example. If anyone has a right to hold a grudge, it would be Him. Why? He was taken, beaten, bruised, mocked, spit at, bloodied, and nailed to a cross all because mankind could not handle losing control over themselves or others. They felt threatened and they did not understand kingdom. However, even in all that Jesus went through, even He chose forgiveness while hanging on the very cross that He was so brutally murdered on, saying before He died, "Father, forgive them, for they know not what they do." Pay attention: If he can forgive for such a brutal crime against Himself, the very Son of God, who are we to believe that we have the right to hold a grudge or unforgiveness against anyone that has done us wrong?

This is not to say that it was easy for Him, or that it should be easy for us! Of course it is not easy, but that does not mean it is impossible! Especially with Papa God!

Another example that we can look at is Joseph. Joseph was Israel's favorite son and everyone knew it. After sharing the dream that God gave him with his family, there was bitterness and jealousy that rose up out of the other brothers. Joseph was put in a pit and sold by his own brothers. This could have caused a lot of anger, hurt, bitterness, and unforgiveness in Joseph's heart, however, we see later on in this story that when Joseph came face to face with his brothers again after gaining status in the palace just below Pharaoh, Joseph never revealed what they did to him out loud. Instead, he protected them. He had so much love and hope for reconciliation with his brothers, that he chose to forgive them for selling his very life.

Now, I don't doubt that this was hard for Joseph, but nevertheless, he loved them through all the hurt they caused him. He loved them because he understood Papa God's heart and saw his brothers from Papa God's perspective rather than of his own. Because of this, the family was reconciled and God created something beautiful out of an ugly situation, all because Joseph understood the power of forgiveness and letting go of control. He trusted that Papa God had it all under control for His glory, His purpose, and that it would all come about in His timing.

I wish I could say that I would have handled these situations the same, and who knows, maybe I would have, or maybe you would, but truth is that the forgiveness I have had to give to various people in my life took me years. Not only did I have to forgive my parents and my Pawpaw along with several others, but I had to go through some major healing and forgiveness with the man that took advantage of me several times as a child and then again at seventeen.

Through the process of forgiving this man I learned a

lot; I learned a lot about myself, I learned that I am strong,.
I learned that it is okay to be angry for a time, I learned
that forgiveness cultivates crazy freedom that I never
want to be without and I learned that it *is* possible to tell
your story without living in your past or being controlled
by those that hurt you.

After going through several months of healing, I was
finally able to let go of unforgiveness and trust that Papa
God was going to take care of it. I was tired of this man
having control over(or the power to speak into) my life.

There is beauty in forgiveness. There is even beauty in
the healing journey although it is most often not a
pleasant trip. This 31 year journey that I have taken had
some dips, bumps, rocks, caverns, mountain tops, valleys,
and even a little bit of death's shadow, but I made it
through and you can too!

Chapter Ten

Walking In True Identity

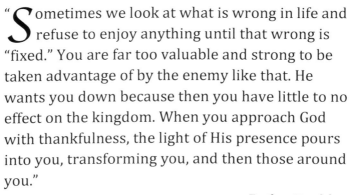

" S ometimes we look at what is wrong in life and refuse to enjoy anything until that wrong is "fixed." You are far too valuable and strong to be taken advantage of by the enemy like that. He wants you down because then you have little to no effect on the kingdom. When you approach God with thankfulness, the light of His presence pours into you, transforming you, and then those around you."

-    Bailey Rushlow

For the longest time this was exactly the way I lived. I believed that I had to have it all figured out, be perfect, or "fix" what was wrong before I could even think about giving myself permission to live freely. The battle for my life has been very real! There are so many times that the enemy tried to destroy my life and on more than one occasion he almost did. Satan almost stole my destiny, my heart, and my future, but he didn't because Papa God wouldn't allow it. I am still here, still breathing, and still running this crazy race! Why? Because Papa God had bigger plans and He has never, one time, let me go!

It's a beautiful thing when you begin to walk in your true identity. Especially when you realize that the very things that were meant to kill you are actually the very things that Papa God uses to catapult you into the destiny he created you for. They are the very things that speak into other people's lives, changes cultures and nations, and sets others free.

**When we begin to walk in our true identity,
freedom and joy are released, atmospheres are
shifted, and it becomes impossible to
live without the presence of Holy Spirit!**

The story of Jacob wrestling with God has always fascinated me! In Genesis 32:24 we see where Jacob wrestled with Him until daybreak. The interesting part about this to me is that Jacob refused to let go of God until he was blessed. Jacob was persistent and stubborn in his pursuit.

Because Jacob wrestled with Him relentlessness, God not only changed his name, but gave him a new identity and shifted the course of his life. God changed his name from Jacob to Israel, from "the Deceiver" to "the one God saves." Jacob's character was changed, and he began to walk fully in who he was created to be.

When we begin to realize that we are not who others say that we are, or who we have believed ourselves to be in the past, but rather who Papa God has called us to be, we begin to see things from a different perspective. This is when freedom takes hold of us in beautiful ways. This is when our life is changed and, like Bailey says, "the light of His presence pours into you, transforming you, and then those around you."

This outpouring of His presence happens because, when we are fully invested in His thoughts about us, we begin to walk in our true identity and it overflows to those around us. And His presence changes everything.

Renewing Your Mind

I learned from a very early age about the concept of "renewing your mind." However, growing up this was not something I held onto, unfortunately. The enemy grabbed a foothold in my life; he manipulated, lied and cheated me out of understanding who I truly am - who I was created to be.

And do not be conformed to this world, but be transformed by the renewing of your mind, so that you

*may prove what the will of God is, that which is good
and acceptable and perfect.*

ROMANS 12:2

Learning to let go, lose control, and allow Holy Spirit to actually do what He wanted in this area of life was not the easiest thing to do. We all like having control. We like having our hands in what takes place in our lives, but the truth is that as long as we have control we are refusing to let Papa God have His way in our lives. This is normally due to a lack of understanding our identity or how much we are loved.

This was my issue. This combined with the fear of even knowing and understanding my identity. I did not know who I was, what my value and worth is to Papa God, and I didn't trust Him to protect me. I feared pursuing the understanding of my identity because it meant I would be held responsible for living life according to His will and not my own. That can be a scary place to be. It's a lot to surrender. It can also be a very beautiful place when you begin to discover the beauty and freedom in it.

Understanding your true identity is recognizing who you belonged to. Recognizing that you are wrapped up in who Papa God says that you are: His. A daughter or a son. Royalty. It took me well into my 20s to begin to really understand this at all.

Growing up, my aunt Angela would tell me constantly how I was "born for such a time as this." She understood the reality of true identity and spoke it over my life continually. To be honest, as badly as I wanted that to be true, to believe her, I couldn't. It seemed impossible to believe that I was who she said I was, or that I would be chosen to live out a life of freedom or significance of any kind. I was a failure and I did not deserve that place. The enemy had me convinced from a very young age that I was nothing but a waste of space, that I rejected these words that she spoke over me. I believed that I was not enough; that I was unworthy of such greatness living inside me. These are the lies that held me hostage into adulthood and kept me deaf to the truth in some pretty big ways.

In my late 20's, I was dating a man that would be the line in the sand as a major defining influence in my life.

We began seeing each other and not long into the relationship, began having sex. I knew better. I knew that what I was doing was not what I was created for, but my belief about myself was still in limbo, and I felt that if I gave him what he wanted then just maybe I could be loved, and just maybe I had found the man that would want to marry me. It wasn't long after this began, however, that Papa God arrested me. He was gentle, but very firm. After wrestling with Him and the feelings of my heart, I gave up. Papa God began to work on my heart in a deeper way and He convinced me that I was worth more than how I was living.

This guy persuaded me to believe that He wanted nothing more than what God had for he and I both. We would sit for hours and have deep and beautiful theological discussions about Papa God and our relationship with Him. We would talk about our dreams and our heart for others. He had me believing that he was the "right one" for me. However, when I sat with him to talk about the things that Papa God had been dealing with me about, everything changed.

"If you love someone, you have sex with them, Kayla!" he said. I knew this was completely false, but for a moment I felt bad, and once again believed the lie that I was not good enough to just simply be with someone outside of anything sexual. Despite this, I told him that it had to stop. He said that if I was not willing to compromise, he was not willing to stay with me.

My response went something like this:

"Well, I'm not willing to compromise and I sure as hell am not willing to be with someone who doesn't see my worth or feel that I'm worth it to wait... someone who doesn't see the worth in waiting and pursuing God's heart over mine!"

And I walked away.

It was in that moment that everything began to change in a way I did not know it could. In the parking lot of that coffee shop, my heart shifted for the first time in a very long time because I made a decision to let Papa God rewire my thoughts and literally renew my mind.

Before this moment, I believed that I was just good

enough for one thing - that I was born to give myself away. I believed the lie that I was only good enough to give people what they wanted until they didn't need me, or until I could provide what they wanted anymore. I believed I wasn't good enough to be kept or to be loved.

Little did I know, even in that moment, that I was born for much more than I could have imagined. Little did I know in that moment that walking away from my own desires would catapult me into my destiny, and that what Angela had been speaking over me my whole life would begin to take shape in my life in even greater ways.

Just to describe briefly, Esther was a common Jewish girl that was taken into the palace of King Xerxes to be prepared as a possible candidate for the replacement of the queen. Queen Vashti was exiled because of defying the king's wishes. Esther was not supposed to be there because of her heritage, but God placed her there strategically, and no one but her uncle Mordecai knew about her true identity.

After being chosen by the king as his bride, Esther faced a situation that could have cost her life. Yet, when it came time to face the king and ask for him to spare her people, the Jews, I can only imagine her reservation and fear, and the questioning of her own ability to do what God had positioned her to do.

Then Mordecai told them to reply to Esther, "Do not imagine that you in the king's palace can escape any more than all the Jews. For if you remain silent at this time, relief and deliverance will arise for the Jews from another place and you and your father's house will perish. And who knows whether you have not attained royalty for such a time as this?"

ESTHER 4:14

Angela, over the years, has reinforced the fact that I am created for right now over and over again. She never gave up, even when I ran. She never gave up when I was using drugs, drinking, lying, hiding, or running. None of that stopped her and I eventually let myself believe her. Could I possibly be born for right now, for such a time as this?!

Once I chose to believe it, I began to believe it deeply. Who I am is not who I have believed my whole life I was. I now truly believe that I am royalty, a daughter of Papa God and the bride of Jesus. I believe this so intensely that I got a tattoo on my left forearm that represents me flying from darkness to royalty, taking on my true identity and living that out.

Here is the thing, we have all been created for royalty - to sit at the right hand of Father with Jesus. You were created for greatness and you were not created to stay silent!

I believe that too often the enemy will slither in like a snake and convince us that our voice is not important, that the things we have to say, to release, is not enough. We let Satan convince us that what we carry is not relevant and that someone else could say it so much better. We believe the lie that we can't, or won't, make a difference or an impact in our generation. That is a bold-faced lie straight from hell.

I spoke about my person a few chapters ago when I spoke about insecurity. This person is also someone that has not only greatly impacted my life but has also set an incredible example of what it means to believe that we are created for purpose. This friend has been molded by God to be a voice for not only her generation but also for the generations before and after her. The things that I have heard her speak about have rocked me in ways that are unexplainable. The revelation that Papa God has given her is meant not only for her, but for the nations, for the generations here now, and the ones to come. She was created a warrior to rock the world. As I said before, If she were to let the enemy silence her, the world would miss out on a beautiful piece of history. But she has refused to let the enemy silence her, and she is now walking out the destiny that papa God has for her – to be a voice for the nations, to the nations.

One of the most beautiful parts of the story of Esther and how she parallels with this beautiful friend of mine is that she was simply chosen to carry out the plans that Papa God had already set to free His people. Esther did not have to be chosen, but she was. God could have chosen anyone out of the multitude of people walking the earth at that time to be the change in history, but He chose Esther to walk out destiny in and with Him. YOU have been chosen to walk out a certain part of history too, and YOU have been chosen to live out your destiny in the identity that Papa God gave you.

Letting Go

When I began to walk in my true identity, people became confused and often uncomfortable. Friends began distancing themselves because they did not understand. Unfortunately, when people do not understand something, they can become judgmental, scared, or fearful of the unknown and do not always react the way that they should.

I have heard the words, "I don't know you anymore" many times. I was constantly asked if this was just temporary, and others told that I was from a different planet.

I often laughed it off but these things are not necessarily easy when coming from a close friend or family. But the truth was, I *was* changing. I was beginning to understand the truth of my reality that I was no longer the person they had always known me to be.

The world will often tell you that you are wrong, that you are not strong enough to carry out what you were created for, or that who you are is just temporary. When we begin to walk in who we were created to be the enemy becomes threatened, and will most often use even the people closest to us to discourage us, put us down, or hurt us until we are at a place of giving up. Yet Colossians 3:2 says to *"Set your mind on the things above, not on the things that are on earth."* By keeping our focus on God, we can persevere through the attacks of the enemy. This is part of renewing our mind daily.

When you do this, you see from heavenly perspective; an eternal perspective rather than your own temporary perspective. You were created for eternal life, not temporary satisfaction. If you live for what man may say about you rather than what Papa God says about you, you will find yourself in a pool of self-doubt, self-hate, and self-righteousness. This focus on self brings about pride which adds a whole new dynamic as life becomes about *you* rather than the One Who created you. Letting go of this control and allowing Papa God to take over and show you His perspective is not easy, but it is possible, and it's worth it!

Let go but DO NOT give up! You were made for more!!

You were made to change the world! You were made to shine! Your past does not define you and others' words and actions do not dictate your present or future, so do not let it! Only Papa God should be defining who we are. As soon as I let go of control and began to understand what I was made for, I ran straight towards Papa God and the destiny He made me for! I have not looked back!

I laugh sometimes at the life I live right now. It is not the easiest by any stretch of the imagination. In fact, it is quite difficult at times, but beautiful nonetheless. I decided to let go of what others have thought, believed, or said about me and chase the God sized dreams that He put in my heart. I am living out my destiny in ways that I never imagined possible.

What is a God size dream?

It is a dream that is far too big for you to ever accomplish on your own. It is the impossible. It is crazy. It is radical. It is uncomfortable. It is something that can only be accomplished by Papa God Himself. Yet He loves partnering with us to make the impossible possible, to bring heaven to earth, and to see broken hearts mended, the sick made well, blind eyes opened, and captives set free!

I have big dreams. I have been told often to pick just one because my dreams are too big and I have too many of them. My response to those questions is, "Why?" Why *not* chase after my God size dreams with Him? Impossibilities are Papa God's specialties! If I have a dream that I feel was a God given dream, why would I limit Him and what He can do? My job, and your job, is to simply say yes, and watch Him do what only He can do!

Because I said yes I am now in Nepal, writing this book, working on research that will eventually carry me places I would not otherwise be able to go. He is getting me ready for the next season of my life in so many ways, teaching me so much about myself, other people, Him, and He and I together. If I had not let Him teach me about my identity and it being solely wrapped up in Him, I would probably still be in the same place I was two, five, or ten years ago, still trying to figure out who I was. But His grace is beautiful, so here I am!

Who Does God Say That You Are?

I want you to journey with me through who He says that you are, because if you can just grab ahold of a little bit of this truth, I promise it will shift your perspective and change both your world and the world of those around you!

Therefore we are ambassadors for Christ, as though God were making an appeal through us; we beg you on behalf of Christ, be reconciled to God.

2 CORINTHIANS 5:20

Behold, My Servant, whom I uphold; My chosen one in whom My soul delights, I have put My Spirit upon Him; He will bring forth justice to the nations.

ISAIAH 42:1

He predestined us to adoption as sons through Jesus

159

Christ Himself, according to the kind intention of His will.

EPHESIANS 1:5

Therefore if anyone is in Christ, he is a new creature; the old things have passed away; behold, new things have come.

2 CORINTHIANS 5:17

And if children, heirs also, heirs of God and fellow heirs with Christ, if indeed we suffer with Him so that we may also be glorified with Him.

ROMANS 8:17

I am the true vine and my Father is the gardener. I am the vine; you are the branches. The one who remains in me--and I in him--bears much fruit, because apart from me you can accomplish nothing.

JOHN 15:1,5

I will give thanks to You, for I am fearfully and wonderfully made; wonderful are Your works, and my soul knows it very well.

PSALM 139:14

Before I formed you in the womb I knew you, and before you were born I consecrated you; I have appointed you a prophet to the nations.

JEREMIAH 1:5

The Lord will make you the head and not the tail, and you will only be above, and you will not be underneath, if you listen to the commandments of the Lord your God, which I charge you today, to observe them carefully.

DEUTERONOMY 28:13-14

But you are a chosen race, a royal priesthood, a Holy nation, a people for God's own possession, so that you may proclaim the excellencies of Him who has called you out of darkness into His marvelous light.

1 PETER 2:9

And who knows whether you have not attained royalty for such a time as this?"

ESTHER 4:14

You, my dear one, were born for such a time as this! You were born at this time for a specific purpose! You were born for great destiny: to shake the nations, ruin hell, set the world on fire, release revival, and bring heaven to earth!

Because you were destined for greatness, the enemy will stop at nothing to take you out. I do not tell you that to scare you! I tell you this to help you see that this is no small thing and so that you may be ready for what is to come.

The beautiful part about this is that YOU WIN! Be prepared, but rest assured that you will not be forsaken.

Jesus already did everything that needs to be done in order to assure your victory! Jeremiah 1:19 says –

They (your enemy) will fight against you, but they will not overcome you, for I am with you to deliver you, declares the Lord.

You see, there is a guarantee that if you will let go of control and step into the identity and the destiny that you were created for, Papa God has your back! In fact, in Jeremiah 2:12, he tells us this – "Then the Lord said to me, "you have seen well, for I am watching over My word to perform it." And in Ezekiel 12:28 God says that *whatever word He speaks will be performed.*

We were born a generation to release revival across the nations! We were created with a voice to wake the dead and to see dry bones come to life! Do NOT lose your voice! Do NOT let the enemy steal your voice or the things that papa God has given you to release over generations! Speak up and release freedom!

Do not wait until you are "fixed" or until you have it all together! Allow Father God to invade your life so that He may invade others through you! Allow Him to heal and restore all that needs to be done in you so that He may work through you in the same way to bring life and restoration to others!

162

The refining process of gold is pretty intense, but it is meant to burn away all impurity! When gold goes through the refining process it is put into the fire and, as the pure gold separates from the impurities, the impurities rise to the top and they are removed by the craftsman. This craftsman will sit next to the hot flames that reach in excess of 1832(°F) to stir and scrape the top to remove the impurities until everything that doesn't belong is burnt out. Much like this process, we are taken through the fire to purify us and get rid of anything that does not belong, making us more beautiful in the end.

Don't be afraid of the fire! The fire is meant to burn away everything that is not of Papa God It is meant to burn away all religion, tradition, anger, hurt, perverse mindsets, false teaching, false doctrine, and anything else that needs to be removed from your life. The refining process is necessary in order for Papa God to invade every part of you, to purify you for the things He has ordained for you. If you will notice, the craftsman sits by the fire and does not leave. Likewise, your Father will not leave you! He is invested in you.

Zechariah gives a beautiful picture of the remnant that God has chosen for His purposes in our lives. In chapter 13, verses 8-9 he says –

It will come about in all the land, declares the Lord, that two parts in it will be cut off and perish; but the third will be left in it. And I will bring the third part through the fire, refine them as silver is refined, and test them as gold is tested. They will call on My name, and I will answer them; I will say, 'they are My people,' and they will say, 'The Lord is my God.'

The third of the land left in this passage is the remnant, those that follow and obey the voice of Father. This is the remnant of a generation that says yes, lets go of control, and runs relentlessly into their destiny to change the world because they understand the urgency of giving their life for the sake of love!

Just as Ezekiel in Ezekiel chapter 37 of the Bible speaks to the valley of bones and they came to life, so you will speak to the nations, to your generations, and to whoever God has for you to encounter, and life will enter them. The very breath of God will be released through you if you will just give Him your "Yes."

Do NOT be afraid to take your place! Do NOT be afraid to take the baton and run the race He has so strategically mapped out for you! You are called, chosen, and capable because of Him through you.

He is remaking you into a people invincible!
(Micah 4:13 MSG)

Chapter Eleven

Possessed by Love

What does it mean to be possessed by love - the very essence of God the creator of the universe? What does it mean to be possessed by the very one that created us to be His?

In being possessed by the very presence of the living God do we find who we are – simply His. It is in being possessed by Him that we learn what true intimacy is all about. It is in communion with Him as the lover of our souls, as the very heartbeat of Father beats in time with our own, and in being entangled by passionate pursuit do we start to learn where we belong: in His heart.

This life is not about what you do or who others think you are. It is not about being on a platform, having a good reputation, popularity, status, or a massive following. It is not about living in the greatest place on earth, living the American dream, or even living as a missionary to pursue the nations for the sake of Love. This life is all about Him and our relationship with Him first and foremost above anything else. It is about pursuing His heart even as He is pursuing ours. Everything else is birthed out of that relationship with Him. But, we have to be willing to lay down everything - our lives, our people, and dreams - and trust that He is going to fulfill the calling and promises He has spoken, even if it is not in our timing.

So, what are you willing to give up or lay down to be fully possessed by the very One who created you, calls you, pursues you, purchased you with His blood, and is relentless in His love for you?

This is the one thing that He asks of us – our heart! But, He is a gentle Father, friend, and lover. He will not force Himself on you. He will not manipulate or coax you into anything. He will simply reveal His heart and give you the choice of life or death, possession by Him or possession by the world.

I want to invite you into an encounter that I had with this beautiful Man not long ago. It was a moment of understanding who I was, who He is, and who we are together. It was a beautiful moment in time – a beautiful love story! This romance literally swept me off my feet and into His arms.

This is my story:

As I sit on the floor of this dark empty room, I wonder if He would come. The carpet is so soft, shaggy and white, my favorite. The walls a light sandy color, just enough color to set the mood for calm. The chairs that normally occupied the floor space are all gone.

As I sit on the floor of this dark empty room, I wonder if He will come.

I feel so alone.

With my eyes tightly shut, the band begins to play and the music – ahhh - it begins to settle my spirit. The band does not even realize I exist. They are just here. Playing. Worshiping. Lost in the melody of their dance with their Creator and it is almost as if they are simply part of the atmosphere.

As I sat in the middle of this floor of this room, eyes still closed, falling into the music, I continue to wonder if He will come.

Suddenly, I feel His hand on my cheek. As I open my eyes, my heart beats faster. I am nervous. He leads my face to look at His. We lock eyes and it's over.

I am not alone.

I had waited for Him. I had waited for Him because it is only when I am with Him that everything else falls away. The insecurities, the fears, the worry, the stress, the shame, the wondering, the doubt, and the anger are no longer an issue and I am now acutely aware of His nearness.

I don't want Him to leave!

He takes a step back, eyes still locked on mine, and He puts His hand out for mine.

"Baby, will you trust Me?" He asks.

He is so gentle, so real. He is the pure and raw definition of True Love. I feel safe. But suddenly fear takes over. Anxiety and insecurity quickly dance their way through my mind.

What if I do give in? What if? Will He let me go, too? Will everything that I give Him be worth the sacrifice? Will giving Him my heart just end up in more broken pieces? Will He let me go as soon as I give Him my hand? Why am I feeling this way? Will He betray me? Why am I struggling to trust Him when He has been nothing but good to me?

As I sit there on the floor scared to give in, to let him

shatter the wall around my heart, I look at Him and plead with tears running down my face, "please don't hurt me anymore than I already have been. Please don't take advantage of me. Please don't let me go if I give you my everything! I don't know how much more I can take. I don't know how much longer I can hold on. I feel so weak, vulnerable, and exposed. I feel so..."

Wait.

What do I feel?

This is different...unfamiliar.

I am no longer sitting on the floor of this dark empty room, wondering if He will come... He is here.
What is happening? This is completely different. He has pulled me into His arms. The music continues to play it is perfect in every way. It is telling our story.

//You steady me, slow and sweet, we sway.
Take the lead and I will follow.
Finally ready now to close my eyes and just believe
that You won't lead me where You don't go.
When my faith gets tired and my hope seems lost,
You spin me round and round and remind me of that
song, the one You wrote for me and we dance.
And I've been told to pick up my sword and fight for

love.
Little did I know that Love had won for me.
Here in Your arms You still my heart again and I
breathe You in like I've never breathed 'till now.
When my faith gets tired and my hope seems lost,
You spin me round and round and remind me of that
song, the one You wrote for me and we dance.
And I will lock eyes with the One who's ransomed me,
the One who gave me joy for mourning
And I will lock eyes with the One who's chosen me,
the One who set my feet to dancing?
We dance just You and me.
It's nice to know I'm not alone, I found my home here
in Your arms.
It's nice to know I'm not alone. I found my home here
in Your arms.
It's nice to know I'm not alone. I found my home here
in Your arms.///

Bethel Music – Steffany Gretzinger

Who is this Jesus? Why does He want me? Does He
know what He is doing... what He is getting Himself into?
Does He know that I am broken, damaged, and unworthy
of Who He is? He is perfect and I am not!

I begin to drown Him in questions.

"Don't you know who I am? Who I have been? What I have done? Don't you remember the times that I purposefully turned my back on you and cursed You to your face? Don't you remember when I looked for other lovers because I said You were not good enough, because I was not good enough for you? Don't you remember when I tried to drown You out with drugs and alcohol? Don't you remember when I blatantly disobeyed you because I hated you? Don't you remember the lies, the manipulation, the nights and days of running and hiding? Don't you remember me hating you? Because I do. I remember it all, and to be honest, I do not have a clue why you would want someone like me! Why would you waste Your time? I am not worth Your time or Your love!

But, He doesn't hesitate for even a moment.

"Yes, I know who you are! I know who I created you to be. I created you with you in mind, with us in mind. I created you with My very hands and with every ounce of My love. I was not surprised by the things you have done or not done. I was not surprised by the fear you faced or your strong will to pursue others or an escape from the life you felt you were drowning in. Do you not understand My love for you goes beyond that? It is unchanging, unwavering, and unconditional.

Don't you remember when you asked me to forgive you? When I said yes, I meant it! So the times that you turned your back, cursed me, searched out other lovers, tried to drown me out with other things, blatantly disobeyed, and even hated me – I don't know what you are talking about. That was forgotten when you came back to Me!

Do you know why I keep you, Kayla? Because you are My beloved, my favorite one. You are chosen, beautiful, and wanted. There is nothing that you can do that will make me love you less and nothing you can do to make me love you more. It is simple. You are mine! You are my beloved. My beautiful one. There is no blemish in you because I have made you clean. You ravish My heart and I will not let you go. I refuse!"

His eyes still held my gaze and He asks me again, "Will you trust Me?"

What is happening to me? I think to myself. My heart is overwhelmed and without a moment of thought or reservation, I yell out "YES!! You can have my yes forever and always!"

It was in this moment that everything that had kept me chained down on that floor was lifted off and healing truly began. You should have seen the look on His face! The biggest and most beautiful smile you have ever seen. He grabs me and tells me to follow His lead and He will take me to places that I have never dreamed.

He met me where I was, He loved me into healing, He

protected and calmed my heart like I had never known before. And we danced. We danced until I fell asleep. It was this day that I began to fall in love, for real, for the first time ever.

This is what true love really looks like – redemption, forgiveness, unconditional acceptance, and pure, raw passion from the One who gave His life for me so that we could dance together forever. This is true love. A passionate pursuit when I did not deserve to be pursued at all.

I will forever give this man, Jesus, my yes. Until the end of time, whatever He wants from me is His. I want to be possessed by Love Himself and see others set free and walk in their true identity and destiny!

Afterword

When Love Takes Over

What would happen if we refused to live any other way but to know the Father's heart to its depth and never moved from the place of intimacy with Him where nothing else mattered? What would happen if what we wanted didn't matter anymore? What would happen if we refused to live any other way but with Him? What would happen if we actually dove into His heart and remained there, refusing to live any other way except in the ebb and flow of that place?

The answer is that we would simply be living the life that He planned the whole time with no heart issues, no questions, no worries, no fears, no guessing, and no wondering, just pure joy and understanding that He literally has our life in His hands.

I think the most beautiful part is this – Papa God doesn't just have our life in His hands but His desire is to dance with us in the greatest way, make the loudest noise ever heard, paint the most vibrant colors ever seen, and sing the most beautiful songs ever sung. He wants to tell the rest of the world that they are loved by their Creator. He wants to see captives free and to bind up the broken hearted. He wants to see lives transformed... and all because of love.

You are all that He says you are. Period.

Acknowledgments

My Jesus – There are no words to express the fullness of what You mean to me! You have saved me from myself in ways that are undeniable and you have saved me from spending eternity without You! Thank you for loving me past my past and for choosing me to speak of Your greatness! I would not be who I am if it were not for Your constant pursuit and love over me! You are my best friend, my lover, my Jesus! I am nothing without You!! I love you passionately and relentlessly!

My beautiful family, thank you for all of your love and support through this process. For believing in me and pushing me in the best ways. You guys mean more to me than I can put into words!

Mom, thank you for loving me the way that you have! I would not be who I am today if it were not for you! Thank you for pushing through life with me and for believing I could and always would be who I was created to be!

Dad, thank you for loving the way you do. Thank you for the long talks and for understanding my crazy, even when I don't myself! Thank you for investing your time and your love regardless of what it cost you and thank you for making up for all the crap times in our lives.

Aaron, thank you for being my best friend growing up and for all the fights and rescues! You have saved my life more times than you could possibly know. You are beyond amazing, bub!

Abby, thank you for always being you and for being someone that has loved me even at my lowest! You never give up and that has kept me holding on more than you will ever know!

I love you guys more than you will EVER know!!
My life would not be the same without you!

Bailey Rushlow! What to say?? Thank you for being you always, first and foremost! Thank you for walking with me through this whole project from start to finish and for believing in me when I questioned myself, even in the slightest bit. Thank you for the hours that you put into this crazy adventure and for the beautiful art work you have done to bring Papa's words to life in a beautiful and deeper way! Your friendship, encouragement, and love has helped me to heal in ways I did not realize I still needed healing and has helped to shape me into an even greater lover of Jesus! You are an inspiration beyond words! To Neverland and back!

Tim and Angela, I cannot put into words what you guys mean to me! Thank you for loving me when I did not feel lovable! Thank you for all of your support, kicks, pushes, encouragement, and the ridiculous and unconditional love you have given me when I did not deserve it! Thank you for loving me beyond myself and for believing in Papa God through me! I love you both more than I can possibly put into words!

Heather Lynn, girl! Thank you for your contribution to this project and for taking on a round of editing! Thank you for believing in me and in what Papa God put together before it was fully birthed! Thank you for investing your time, heart, prayers! You're amazing!

Clara Starr! Thank you for investing your heart, time, and brain into this project! Thank you for all the hours of editing to help shape it in an even greater way!! :) You are incredible beyond words!

A special and deep thank you to some of my college instructors – **Paula Dixon, Jennifer Lester-Benson, and Blake Rackley** – for all of the wisdom, support, and encouragement during my 4 years at Emmanuel and way beyond! Your friendship and love kept me during one of the craziest times of my life! I am who I am in large part due to you and Papa God through you! I love you guys and I thank you for loving me beyond your job! You are AMAZING!!!

Thank you, **Alissa Buerline**! For the many hours of grueling dedication you put towards pursuing crazy healing and pushing me when I wanted to quit! Thank you for your love and support and seeing me through literally the hardest time of my life! I definitely would not be the person I am if it were not for you and your yes to Papa God!! I have loved in ways I never knew I could, been loved in ways I never knew were possible, have experienced freedom I did not know was available, and I have laughed more in the last two years than I have in all of my life! Thank you for being your amazing self and for your dedication to seeing others healed in such deep-rooted ways! You are the Best. Counselor. Ever!

To my amazing BFA Nepali women! You have made my life so much richer and to say thank you is hardly sufficient enough to explain the impact that you have had on my life! You have taught me what it means to love past barriers. Thank you for laughing with me, dancing with me, and for loving me in ways that have taken my heart to a deeper place in Papa God's heart. Don't ever forget your worth or your purpose and never stop chasing after destiny! You are beautiful, chosen, wanted, and relentlessly pursued by Papa God and He will stop at nothing to have and keep you! I love you!!

To the other beautiful people in my life (friends and family) that have stood by my side, believed in me, supported me (in EVERY way), and loved me through the good, bad, ugly, and beautiful, I love you!! You are such a huge part of my history - past, present, and future and I could not be more grateful and honored to have you part of my life!

Notes

Chapter 1
1. Isaiah 61:1-4.
2. Proverbs 2:11.
3. Genesis 50:20.
4. Joel 2:25.

Chapter 2
1. Matthew 5:48.
2. 1 John 3:2-3.
3. John 13:35.
4. Matthew 7:7-8.
5. Luke 11:9.

Chapter 3
1. Luke 10:38-42.
2. Psalm 139:13-16.
3. Hebrews 10:24-25.

Chapter 4
1. John 8:34-36.
2. Psalm 139:13-16.
3. Hebrews 10:24-25.

Chapter 5
1. Ephesians 6:10-13.
2. Romans 1:26.
3. 1 Corinthians 6:9.
4. 1 Timothy 1:8-10.
5. 1 Corinthians 6:18.

Chapter 6
1. 1 Corinthians 11:2.
2. Romans 12:2.
3. Isaiah 52:12.
4. Revelation 12:11.
5. Zephaniah 3:17.
6. Psalm 139:7-11.
7. 2 Corinthians 12:10.
8. Jesus Culture – "Pursuit" lyrics.

Chapter 7
1. Isaiah 61:7.
2. Psychology Today – Dr. Joseph Burgo: p 107.

BAILEY RUSHLOW

How do you describe someone who loves you through the good, bad, and ugly and still chooses you? How do you describe the person that fights with you in the trenches, battles on the front lines, loves through the mess and rejoices with you on the mountain tops? How do you describe the woman that would give her life for the one next to her?

She is a warrior, a fighter. She embodies Love itself! She is love with skin on.

Here is a woman that loves beyond herself and not for anything that she gets out of it but, because Papa God has given her His heart to love others beyond their understanding. Not only does she do this in relationships, but she releases it in her music, in the way she speaks, her writing, and her life.

I tell you about Bailey because without her, without her existence, this world would be a very different place. She not only lives in and carries the presence of Holy Spirit, but she releases Him everywhere He goes just simply by being her. She understands the importance of simply being who she was created to be. She understands the urgency of not only walking in relationship with Papa God, but in releasing what she carries as well. More than pushing boundaries or striving to be someone she is not, she lives every day as though it is the only one that matters. She lives an authentic, real, and vulnerable life.

She changes the world. Papa God changes the world through her.

Bailey is a musician, singer, writer, speaker, a best friend, beautiful daughter, and an amazing human who has a voice that needs to be heard!

To experience the Bailey that those who have met her know, check out her links below! You will experience something and someone beautiful in Bailey Rushlow.

Email: bailey.rushlow@gmail.com
Facebook: baileynrushlow
Twitter: @baileynrushlow
Instagram: @baileynrushlow
YouTube: Bailey Rushlow
Patreon: www.patreon.com/baileynrushlow
ReverbNation: www.reverbnation.com/baileynrushlow

BRANDED COLLECTIVE

Why The Branded Collective?

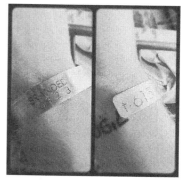

While so many are called to serve in other areas or overseas, The Branded Collective has a heart and a passion to fight the battle of human trafficking in their home of Nashville, Tennessee. It is a response to give a voice to those that have been silenced and giving back in opportunity that human trafficking survivors may not otherwise have.

The BRANDED Collective works closely with another Nashville-based non-profit organization, End Slavery Tennessee. The mission is to employ survivors of human trafficking and give them the chance to break loose of the statistical mold and live a life of worth and dignity that they were created for to begin with.

Because many human trafficking victims are literally branded, The Branded Collective has decided to fight from another perspective of being branded. The beautiful idea of the BRANDED concept is to *"Become a number to restore a name."* Each individual and handcrafted piece contains a unique number to represent one of the millions of beautiful faces and names of those trapped in human trafficking.

The "Collective" is a group of us that have come together and decided to stand for those beautiful people who have been rescued and those still trapped in the nightmare of trafficking.

Band together with us to "wear the story, share the story, and change the story." Join us in changing the world one piece of jewelry, one story, & one heart at a time!

To learn more about how you can become a voice and a part of The Branded Collective, check out their website and join the mission to change the world.

Website: www.brandedcollective.com
Facebook: @brandedcollective
Twitter: @BRANDED_co
Instagram: @brandedcollective

Made in the USA
Columbia, SC
30 October 2017